SOLVING FINANCIAL ACCOUNTING
USING EXCEL FOR WINDOWS

to accompany

FINANCIAL
ACCOUNTING

Fourth Edition

REX A SCHILDHOUSE M.B.A., C.M.A.
University of Phoenix – San Diego Campus
San Diego, California

JERRY J. WEYGANDT Ph.D., C.P.A.
Arthur Andersen Alumni Professor of Accounting
University of Wisconsin - Madison
Madison, Wisconsin

DONALD E. KIESO Ph.D., C.P.A.
KPMG Peat Marwick Emeritus Professor of Accountancy
Northern Illinois University
DeKalb, Illinois

PAUL D. KIMMEL Ph.D., C.P.A.
Associate Professor of Accounting
University of Wisconsin - Milwaukee
Milwaukee, Wisconsin

JOHN WILEY & SONS, INC.

COVER PHOTO   © Bill Ross/CORBIS.

To order books or for customer service call 1-800-CALL-WILEY (225-5945).

ISBN 0-471-20531-1

Printed in the United States of America

10 9 8 7 6 5 4 3 2 1

Printed and bound by Victor Graphics, Inc.

NOTE TO THE INSTRUCTOR

The Weygandt *Financial Accounting 4/e* Excel Workbook templates are available in two formats that will meet your particular needs. The first format is the format found on the CD attached to this booklet. This format provides basic guidance in solving the exercises and problems and contains keys for account title placement, value placement, and formula placement. This format is intended to provide your students a structured environment to reduce the time required to accomplish the exercise or problem without reducing the educational challenge and opportunity afforded by exercise or problem. Very few account titles and no account values are given in this format. The student template contains an instructions worksheet and an area for the student to identify him or herself, the course, the due date, and the instructor. The exercise or problem identification is near the top of the first page of every exercise or problem. Each template is also set up with footers stating the exercise or problem identity, the page number of page numbers, and the time printed to assist in compiling the many pages you may receive.

The second format is a "partially populated" exercise or problem format where, in addition to the standard format described above, some account titles and account values are given to the student to assist in solving the exercise or problem. These are available to you for distribution as downloads from the Weygandt Finanical 4/e Instructor's Resources web site. This format contains the same problem presentation as the first format.

Solutions for both types of templates are available on the Weygandt *Financial Accounting 4/e* Instructor's web site and CD. Each solution template contains the instruction sheet given to the student, the exercise or problem as given to the student, and the solution. The solution template matches the placement of data in the student template and is very closely correlated to the text book solutions manual. This format is intended to assist you in the evaluation of the student's accomplishments without presenting an alternative to textbook presented methodology or the solutions manual materials.

INTRODUCTION

This booklet is written to accompany the Fourth Edition of Weygandt, Kieso, and Kimmel's Financial Accounting, fourth edition text book. Throughout the booklet numerous subjects are addressed under the title of Clues, Hints, and Tips, which are intended to increase your ability and skills in using Microsoft Excel or most other spreadsheet applications in the accomplishment of academic and professional tasks. Many of the later chapters assume that you fully understand and have mastered the skills presented in the earlier chapters. Because of this assumption, it is recommended that even proficient users of Excel read the booklet as they accomplish the assigned work.

The templates were constructed in Microsoft Excel XP. The files should be accessible from Excel 5.0 and Excel 95 up to, and including, Excel XP (Excel 2002). The majority of commands and capabilities are common to many of the various versions of Excel as well as other spreadsheet applications.

Each chapter of this booklet also contains the complete exercise or problem for which an Excel template has been provided. The exercises and problems are preformatted on the computer media that accompany the booklet. Each exercise or problem is identified with its own file name. For Exercise E1-4, the fourth exercise within Chapter 1 the file name is 1e-4 on the computer media. Problem P1-2A has the file name 1p-2a while Problem P1-4B would have the file name 1p-4b.

Many of the chapters have additional data files associated with them to further show or demonstrate the capabilities of Excel. The data file for Chapter 1 would be titled chptr1 on the computer media. The Excel worksheet tabs have been labeled in many of the workbooks to make the selection of the appropriate worksheet easier.

Numerous screen prints have been included to clarify the presentation of the material. If you need assistance on a particular issue you can also accomplish the screen print function and take the document into the classroom, to your information technologies assistance center, or attach it to an email. To perform a screen print most reliably, first, open the application that you wish to receive the screen print. This application is usually Microsoft Word and will be used for the explanation. Then return to the application or screen that you want to screen print. Press the "Screen Print" key on the keyboard. This key is usually just above the Insert key on the keyboard but may be anywhere on the keyboard. The image of the screen is now held on the Windows Clipboard. Reselect the receiving application, Word in this case, click into an open document to place the cursor and use the key strokes Ctrl-V or click the "Paste" icon and the image should be pasted into the document. Now you can save the document as a file for later use and/or print it to show later or to document an event. Applications such as Microsoft Word, Windows WordPad, Windows Paint, Microsoft Excel, and Microsoft Access all accept screen prints. Windows Notepad does not accept screen prints.

CHAPTER 1

ACCOUNTING IN ACTION

CHAPTER OUTLINE

CLUES, HINTS, AND TIPS

General

Clues, hints and tips will be provided throughout the booklet. Microsoft Excel is a very powerful tool that is extremely easy to control. Exposure to Excel will be a growing process. The more you utilize Excel and become familiar with it, the more you will accomplish with it. It is recommended that a note pad be started to document useful information about Excel in an easy to find presentation. Various help screens can be printed for later reference. Placing notes about the issue addressed on the printout may be helpful later. Excel can be utilized to accomplish many of the exercises and problems throughout the text book by creating your own worksheets. Check with your instructor to ensure that Excel worksheets are acceptable for the accomplishment of exercises and problems where templates have not been provided.

    Several general subject areas of Excel are presented to assist you with your homework.

Opening Excel

To open Microsoft Excel, double-click the icon on the desktop of Windows labeled Shortcut to Excel. If there is no icon, look for the Microsoft Office Shortcut Bar usually found at the top of the screen. You may also find the Excel execute file (.exe) by using Windows Explorer. To open Explorer, double-click on the Explorer icon on the screen. On a desktop system, single click on the "Disk C" line. If there is a plus (+) next to this line, click on the plus once to expose all folders/directories on the left side of the display. If Explorer fills the screen or prevents you from seeing the desktop area, use the Maximize/Minimize button (two overlaying sheets) in the upper right corner to reduce its size. Follow the path of Start>Search and select the All Files or Folders option. This will invoke a pop-up dialog box. Within the text entry area labeled "All or part of a file name:" enter "Excel.exe" and click "Search". Search should locate one or more files meeting the criteria. The target file is the file with the large green X in the box on the left of the listing. Single-click the left area (the "X" or the title area) of the one file with the large blue/green "X," labeled Excel with the type of file identified as shortcut or application. Wait a moment then right-click and hold the right mouse button down. Now drag the mouse cursor to the desktop. When positioned over the desktop, release the mouse button. You will be given several options including "Create Shortcut(s) Here" from another pop-up menu. Select the "Create Shortcut(s) Here" option to create a new shortcut to Excel. Once the operation is complete, you should be able to double click this icon on your desktop to open Excel from the desktop.

This is the presentation of Excel's execute file in Explorer:

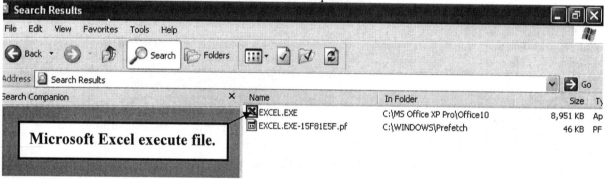

Microsoft Excel execute file.

Opening Excel Files

The templates are recorded on the CD-ROM accompanying this booklet. These should be copied to a directory on the "C" drive or hard drive.

__Note: Do not do this procedure on a computer lab or networked computer.__ If the computer to be used is a computer lab or networked computer, the files should be copied to floppy disks in groups of 4~5 chapters to a floppy disk.

To do this:

1.   Open Windows Explorer.
2.   Insert the CD-ROM disk into the CD drive of the computer.
3.   Locate the CD drive in Windows Explorer and double click it so the file directory of "Fin Acctg 4th ed templates" is showing on the right side of the Windows Explorer pane.
4.   Adjust the left side of the Windows Explorer pane to show the C Drive.
5.   Left click once onto the "Fin Acctg 4th ed templates" on the right side of the Windows Explorer pane.
6.   With the left mouse button still depressed, drag the directory to the C drive or the hard drive shown in the left side of the Windows Explorer pane.

7. Windows Explorer may present you with a pop-up menu asking you your desires. Select "Copy here" from the options and Windows Explorer will copy the entire directory from the CD-ROM to the hard drive. From that point on the data files for the booklet will be stored and available on the "Fin Acctg 4th ed templates" directory of your hard drive.

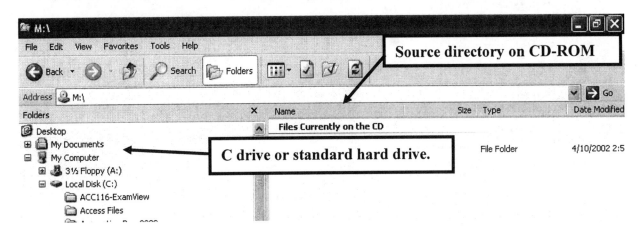

This screen print shows the source directory on the CD-ROM disk and the C drive or the standard hard drive on the computer.

To open the template 1e-4, (for Chapter 1, Exercise 4), open Excel, click on the Open File icon (an opening file), follow the path File>Open, or utilize the keystrokes Ctrl-O (letter "O" for open in upper or lower case). When presented with the Open File dialog box, use the drop-down arrow on the right side of the Look In window to expose all of the drives available. Locate and select the C drive or the hard drive that contains the "Fin Acctg 4th ed templates" directory by clicking the left mouse button once. The displayed files will change to those of the Fin Acctg 4th ed templates" directory. Use the slide bars on the bottom or side of the display to move the display until you locate the file titled 1e-4. When located, double clicking the target file, 1e-4, will open the file immediately without further action. Clicking it once will require the Open button on the right side of the dialog box to be clicked as well. The template will load automatically into the display.

To move around the template you can use the arrow keys, Page Up/Down, Tab, Enter or click the left mouse button while the cursor is over the target cell. Alphabetical characters or numerical values can be entered into a cell simply by typing them in. If an entry starts with an arithmetic function symbol (=, /, *, + or -), preceding it with a single apostrophe (') will force Excel to read it as text. Otherwise an error message may appear in the cell unless it is a proper formula.

To save the data, click the Save icon (a 3.5" floppy disk icon) on the toolbar, follow the path File>Save or utilize the keystrokes Ctrl-S. All of these actions will use the default location and name—where it was opened from and it's opening name—to save the file. If you desire to save the file elsewhere or with a new name follow the path File>Save As. This will bring up the Save As dialog box and allow you to assign a new name and/or designate a new save location. This dialog box will also appear when you save a newly created workbook for the first time.

This screen print shows the default directory on the C drive or the hard drive and the target file (example) of 1e-4.

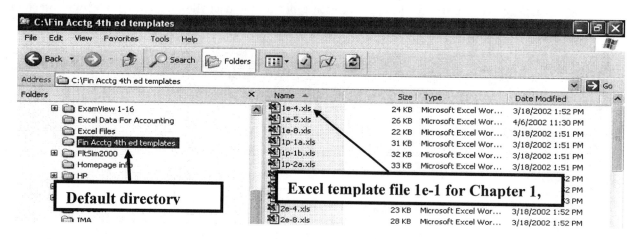

Demo File

Within the data directory there is a demonstration file of Excel basics. This file, called Demo File, has quick and easy examples of how Excel can assist you in accomplishing the exercises and problems. The Demo File shows how the "Look-to" formula works and how it can be integrated into your work. Because you can do "add-ons" to the look-to formula you can utilize this to do math within the templates such as calculate the interest due on a note payable. It is suggested that you open this file, read the Information tab and Instructions tab and then study the Demo File tab itself. This gives an example of a fully completed process of reading the presented material, entering it into a structured general journal, posting the transactions into a ledger, and then creating a trial balance. Very little of this was accomplished through direct entry typing. The extensive use of the look-to formula also reduces the probability of keying errors. The templates have been set up slightly different than the text book so that the look-to formula could be used extensive throughout the exercises and problem. Advanced formulas such as concatenate are utilized in the demo file. These are explained later in the booklet.

One of the features shown in the demonstration file is the split screen presentation of Excel. This is fully explained later in the booklet. It is a useful tool since you can maintain the presentation of the data of the exercise or problem in the upper pane while working in the bottom. Each pane moves independently and you can reference or look-to the other pane while working. This feature will save time and allow you to maintain your orientation while solving the exercises and problems.

Pop-up Menus

Excel will frequently respond to an action with a pop-up menu. This menu seems to appear out of nowhere and be anchored to nothing in particular. Usually it is associated with the currently active object. The most common pop-up menu is the one associated with the active cell, shown below:

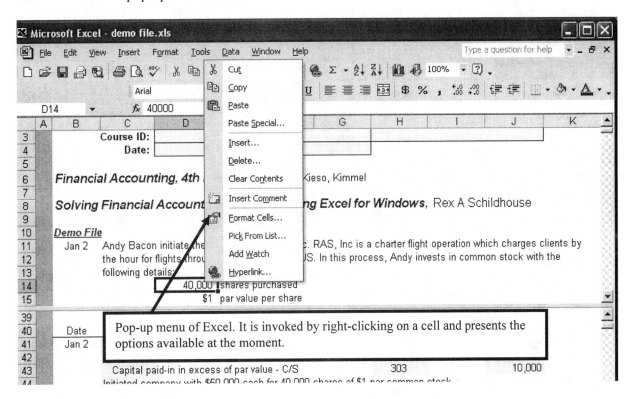

This particular pop-up menu displays the most common commands for the active cell including cut, copy, paste, format cell and insert comment. All of these commands are available through other paths but the action of right clicking the cell or range of cells to gain access to this pop-up menu is the quickest. Pop-up menus are not anchored to an specific item as drop-down menus are.

Drop-down Menu

The drop-down menu is visibly associated with another item such as the "File" title on the menu bar. The drop-down menu from the file title shown below provides access to common file commands like new worksheet, open or close a worksheet, save a worksheet or the save as function for a worksheet, page setup and print area. Many of these will be utilized in this course. Drop-down menus can be accessed by clicking on their titles or striking the Alt key and then using the arrows to move left and right as well as up and down through the menus. Using your mouse to click or double a choice or striking the enter key will normally invoke the highlighted selection. Striking the escape key will normally back you out of the menu without any action taken. This is the appearance of the drop down menu from the file title on the menu bar:

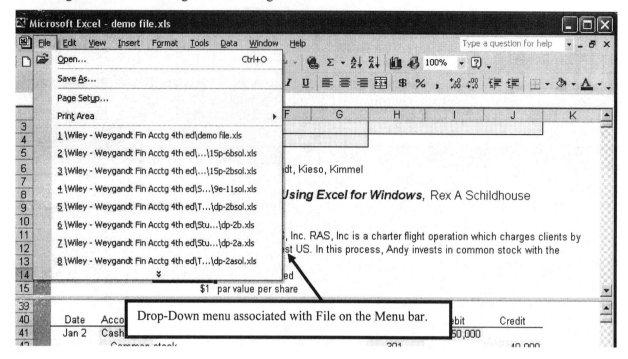

Drop-Down menu associated with File on the Menu bar.

New Workbook

In the process of accomplishing your work with the templates you may want an area to do "scratch" work not to be incorporated into the finished template or file. This can easily be accomplished by opening up a new workbook within Excel. To open the new workbook click once on the clear white sheet with the upper right corner folded over on the taskbar or follow the path File>New. Both will open the new workbook. Excel will normally assign the new workbook a title like Book 2 or Book 3 upon opening. To switch between the workbooks click on Windows on the menu bar and select the worksheet you want to be active from the list at the bottom. If more than can be displayed are available the last line will inform you of that and clicking on that line will display them. By using the Maximizing/Minimizing buttons near the upper right corner of the display you can have more than one workbook showing at the same time even if they overlap. The active workbook will come to the forefront of the display. All commands issued to Excel while two or more books are open will only be effective on the active workbook. Commands such as copy, paste and format painting are available from one workbook to another while they are open. The title bar of Excel will reinforce the active workbook by showing the name.

EXERCISES

Exercise E1-4 (File 1e-4) Analyze transactions and compute net income

A tabular analysis of the transactions made by Kathy Goggin & Co., a certified public accounting firm, for the month of August is shown below. Each increase and decrease in stockholders' equity is explained:

	Cash	+	A/R	+	Supplies	+	Office Equip	=	A/P	+	SHE	
1	18,000										+18,000	Investment
2	(2,000)						+5,000		+3,000			
3	(750)				+750							
4	8,000		+3,400								+11,400	Fees earned
5	(1,500)								(1,500)			
6	(2,500)										(2,500)	Dividends
7	(650)										(650)	Rent expense
8	450		(450)									
9	(2,900)										(2,900)	Salaries expense
10									+900		(900)	Utilities expense

A/R – Accounts receivable   A/P – Accounts payable   SHE – Stockholders' equity
Values in (Parenthesis) are negatives.

Instructions:
  (a) Describe each transaction that occurred for the month.
  (b) Determine how much stockholders' equity increased for the month.
  (c) Compute the amount of net income for the month.

Exercise E1-5 (File 1e-5) Prepare an income statement, retained earnings statement, and a balance sheet.

The tabular analysis of the transactions made by Kathy Goggin & Co. is presented in E1-4.

Instructions:
Prepare an income statement and a retained earnings statement for August and a balance sheet at August 31, 2002.

Exercise E1-8 (File 1e-8) Prepare an income statement and retained earnings statement.

The following information relates to George Pucci Co. for the year 2002.

Common stock, Jan 1, 2002	$45,000	Advertising expense	$1,800
Dividends	6,000	Rent expense	10,400
Service revenues	62,000	Utilities expense	4,600
Salaries expense	28,000		

Instructions:
After analyzing the data, prepare an income statement and a retained earnings statement for the year ended December 31, 2002. Beginning retained earnings was $10,000.

PROBLEMS

Problem P1-1A (File 1p-1a) Analyze transactions and compute net income.

On April 1, Crossroads Travel Agency, Inc. was established. The following transactions were completed during the month:
1. Stockholders invested $20,000 cash, receiving common stock in exchange.
2. Paid $800 cash for April office rent.
3. Purchased office equipment for $2,500 cash.
4. Incurred $300 of advertising costs in the Chicago Tribune, on account.
5. Paid $750 cash for office supplies.
6. Earned $12,000 for services rendered: Cash of $3,000 is received from customers, and the balance of $9,000 is billed to customers on account.
7. Paid $500 cash dividends.
8. Paid Chicago Tribune amount due in transaction (4).
9. Paid employees' salaries, $1,500.
10. Cash of $7,000 is received from customers who have previously been billed in transaction (6).

Instructions:
(a) Prepare a tabular analysis of the transactions using the following column headings: Cash, Accounts receivable, Supplies, Office equipment, Accounts payable, Common stock, and Retained earnings.
(b) From the analysis of the retained earnings column, compute the net income or net loss for April.

Problem P1-5A (File 1p-5a) Determine financial statement amounts and prepare retained earnings statements.

Financial statement information about four different companies is as follows:

	Judd Co.	Hefel Co.	Marpe Co.	Morgan Co.
January 1, 2002				
Assets:	$92,000	$110,000	(g)	$160,000
Liabilities:	50,000	(d)	75,000	(j)
Stockholders' equity	(a)	60,000	57,000	90,000
December 31, 2002				
Assets	(b)	150,000	200,000	(k)
Liabilities:	55,000	68,000	(h)	80,000
Stockholders' equity	58,000	(e)	130,000	162,000
Stockholders' equity changes				
In the year:				
Additional investments	(c)	12,000	10,000	15,000
Dividends	25,000	(f)	14,000	20,000
Total revenues	347,000	420,000	(j)	530,000
Total expenses	320,000	385,000	350,000	(l)

Instructions:
(a) Determine the missing amounts.
(b) Prepare the retained earnings statement for Judd Company. Assume that the beginning balance of retained earnings was zero.
(c) Write a memorandum explaining the sequence for preparing financial statements and the interrelationship of the retained earnings statement to the income statement and the balance sheet.

Problem P1-1B (File 1p-1b) Analyze transactions and compute net income.

On May 1, Brad Pitt Inc was started. A summary of May transactions is presented below:
1. Stockholders invested $20,000 cash in Fox Valley Bank in the name of the business.
2. Purchased equipment for $5,000 cash.
3. Paid $600 cash for May rent.
4. Paid $500 cash for parts and supplies.
5. Incurred $300 of advertising costs in the Beacon News on account.
6. Received $6,500 in cash from customers for repair service.
7. Paid dividends of $500.
8. Paid part-time employee salaries of $1,000.
9. Paid utility bills of $240.
10. Provided repair service on account to customers, $750.
11. Collected cash of $150 for services billed in transaction (10).

Instructions:
(a) Prepare a tabular analysis of the transactions, using the following column headings: Cash, Accounts receivable, Supplies, Equipment, Accounts payable, Common stock, and Retained earnings. (Use the term Service revenue to indicate revenue.)
(b) From an analysis of the Retained earnings column, compute the net income or net loss for May.

Problem P1-4B (File 1p-4b) Prepare income statement, retained earnings statement, and balance sheet.

On June 1, Fritz' Garage, Inc was started with an investment in the company of $26,200 in cash. Following are the assets and liabilities of the company at June 30 and the revenues and expenses for the month of June:

Cash	$11,700	Notes payable	$13,000
Accounts receivable	4,900	Accounts payable	1,400
Service revenue	8,400	Supplies expense	1,200
Auto supplies on hand	2,400	Gas and oil expense	1,000
Advertising expense	500	Utilities expense	300
Equipment	25,000		

No additional investments were made in June, but dividends of $2,000 were paid during the month.

Instructions:
Prepare an income statement and retained earnings statement for the month of June and a balance sheet at June 30, 2002.

CHAPTER 2

THE RECORDING PROCESS

CHAPTER OUTLINE

CLUES, HINTS, AND TIPS

Help

The Help menu of Excel is very useful and gives you several options under the path of Help. Each version of Excel has its own methodology of presenting help so one explanation will not address all situations. One method of attaining help within Excel is by striking the F1 key, the standard help key in a Windows environment. The alternative option is to follow the path Help from the menu bar. Both of these will present you with a dialog box or an office assistant. With this dialog box open, you type in your question, problem, or desired action and click on search, okay, or enter as appropriate. When Excel presents you with a solution, you will need to evaluate it before implementing the proposed solution. If you like the solution, you can print it out for record keeping and reference later on. If Excel cannot find an exact match, it will present you with several options to choose from. If Excel cannot find a match or has no idea of your question, it will ask that you rephrase the question. Your best responses come from active tense questions. If your first effort does not provide a reasonable response, try changing the question. For example, if you are trying to format a header, typing "Header" into the help menu will result in one array of options. However, entering "Format headers" will present a different array of headers. The Microsoft homepage at www.microsoft.com has additional help and assistance options. Some versions of Excel will ask if you want to continue your data search on the internet and the homepage. An alternative is to change the plurals to singulars and the singulars to plurals in your query.

Command Access

Excel has numerous command paths to accomplish almost every one of its many commands. The selection and utilization is up to you. If you are a proficient typist, you may select keyboard commands while typing and mouse commands while doing graphic tasks. Others will always select the mouse while some will use the "Alt" or Alternate" key path.

The most common method of accessing Microsoft Excel commands is through the mouse. With this concept, you would select a word on the menu bar by placing the mouse cursor over it and clicking on it. A drop-down menu would appear, attached to the menu bar, with the options available at the point in time and in relation to that position on the worksheet. If an item is grayed out or faded, it is not available for some reason. You would then select the desired option by clicking on it with the mouse. If the option has an arrowhead pointing to the right or left, that selection has other choices available to it and selecting it or placing the cursor over it will result in an expanded display for that selection. Once shown, clicking on the desired option will result in its selection. If no selection is found or you decide you are in the wrong path, clicking anywhere other than on the drop-down menu will back you out without a selection being activated. You may also strike the "Esc" or escape key to cancel the menu and avoid a selection. Using the menu bar method, the copy command is Edit>Copy.

The second methodology of selecting commands it to use keyboard commands. With the use of a predecessor key such as the Control key or Alternate key, other options become available with additional key strokes. For example, to copy something using keyboard commands, activate the cell, the press and hold the Control key down and the strike and release the "C" key. The shift key is not hit and it does not matter if the keyboard is locked into upper or lower case at the time. Once the "C" key is stroke, the keys can be released in any order. This type of keyboard command will be addressed and identified as "Ctrl-C" throughout the booklet.

An alternative is to use the "Alt" key or Alternate key to access the menu bar. By striking this key you will see the first item on the menu bar become active. By using the arrow keys to move left and right as well as up and down, you can prowl the menu bar for your selection. When located, striking the "Enter" key will select and activate the command you have chosen.

Regardless of the method you have used to access the command structure of Excel, the Esc or Escape key will usually back you out of the command path without making a selection. It may take one or more strikes of the escape key to accomplish the back-out.

Copying and pasting

Excel allows you to copy and paste both cells and data from within cells. Both of these functions can be used in accomplishing the tasks of the templates. The first function to be addressed is copying a cell. This function is accomplished by activating the cell you would like to copy. To do this, select it in any way you desire. The options are put your mouse cursor over it and click into it, use the arrow keys to move your current selected cell over to the desired cell, strike the tab key, or strike the enter key. When striking the enter key, the cursor will move as controlled by the options set under the edit tab of the options dialog box. This tab can be found by following the path Tools>Options>Edit from the menu bar. The active cell can be identified by the heavy or accented outline such as cell 6 in the presentation here:

1	2	3	4
5	6	7	8
9	10	11	12
13	14	15	16

A range may be selected by sweeping it with the cursor while the left mouse button is being held down. In this case, the range selected will be highlighted such as cells 25, 26 and 27 as shown here:

21	22	23	24
25	26	27	28
29	30	31	32
33	34	35	36

Once a cell or range of cells is selected, you can copy it by clicking on the two overlaying sheets of paper on the task bar, by right clicking the cell or cells and selecting the copy command from the pop-up menu, or by following the path Edit>Copy. You can also utilize the keyboard command of Control key down and striking the "C" key. This type of command is presented as Ctrl-C throughout the booklet. When copied, the cell or range of cells is carrying its formatting details with it. This feature is very convenient since you would normally want copied data to be presented in the same manner as the original presentation. The data is now in your clipboard and ready for pasting. Move your cursor to the desired pasting location and click on the clipboard icon on the task bar, right click on the cell and select the paste command from the pop-up menu, or follow the path Edit>Paste.

If you selected more than one cell, the group or range of cells copied will be pasted in the same orientation as those from the upper, left most cell of the selection. When pasting, if you have selected a cell or range of cells containing data, Excel will not warn you that you are pasting over data. The existing data will be overridden by the paste operation. However, all is not lost – you can use the Undo command to recover the data. When working with Microsoft Office XP or 2002 products such as Excel XP or Excel 2002, there may be more than one item on the clipboard at a time. To view the various items on the clipboard follow the path Edit>Office Clipboard and the items on the clipboard will be displayed. The clipboard function will hold up to 24 objects from any of the Microsoft Office products registered to the system so you can open up Word, copy multiple items out of a document, open up Excel and paste those items as you desire. The clipboard will retain its contents through save operations and, as stated, it displays all of the information from all of the registered products allowing it to be used as an import/export tool for multiple items.

Undo and Redo

With the versatility of Excel and the Microsoft Office Products, errors are bound to occur due to the capability to manipulate data. When going to copy a cell and using keyboard commands of Control-C, the keystrokes of Ctrl-V may be struck instead resulting in a paste operation rather than a copy operation. To correct this event utilize the curling to the left blue arrow on the task bar. Clicking directly on it will reverse the last action taken. There is a drop-down menu selection available with undo through the small arrow pointing down just to the right of the symbol. With the selection of one of the events depicted you can reverse not the last event but an event that occurred 3, 4 or 5 errors ago. In older versions of Excel, the save function will preclude undo's from the period prior to the undo.

Redo will reinstate an undo action. This icon is a blue sweeping arrow to the right, a mirror image of the undo arrow. It also has a drop-down menu associated with it to select prior events.

These two arrows/icons are shown here:

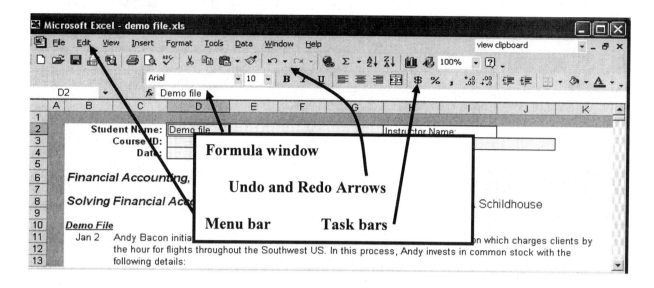

Saving Excel Files

The motto of "Save early and save often" of days gone by of desktop computing are not lost with today's increased reliability. Excel offers numerous ways to save a file. The most common is to simply click on the 3.5 disk icon on the task bar. This will save the file back to its original source making it easy to locate a second time or for later use. This may be done with the Excel templates accompanying this booklet. You can also use the keyboard command Ctrl-S to invoke the save command. An alternative is using the menu bar path of File>Save.

When using save the file is copied back to its original source in the original format. If either of these desires changes, you can impose that change on Excel. For example, you want to save it to your hard drive, your "C" drive in the Excel Files directory and you using a floppy disk as a source. By following the path File>Save As a dialog box is opened which allows you to change the location by modifying the presentation of the "Save in" box near the top of the dialog box, you can change the name of the file in the lower portion of the box through the "File name" window and you can change the type of file through the selection in the "Save as" type window at the bottom of the dialog box. These options give you great power over your data. You can open the file on a floppy and save it to the hard drive, a network drive, or other storage devices you may have available. You can change the name from the default established by Microsoft Excel from Book 1 to a more desirable and descriptive title allowing easier relocating the correct file and you may change its type to allow it to opened by other, less sophisticated software packages.

In selecting the name for the file there are a few special characters that cannot be used. These include most of the characters above the numbers on the keyboard and several others. The availability of characters is ample. It is also a good idea to date files that are used often. This allows you to simple back up and recovery if something goes awry. For example, you are using Excel to keep your checkbook and each day you enter the checks and transactions into the file called Checks. By modifying the title to include Friday's date each week you will retain the previous week's data even if this week's file is lost. And since the dash or hyphen and spaces are legal characters within a file title you can label the file "Checks 1-04-02" for the first Monday of January 2002. The following Friday using File>Save as you would modify the file name to "Checks 1-11-02". The file "Checks 1-4-02" is still in the directory if "Checks 1-11-02" is no longer available for some reason.

You can also change the file type to a text type, comma delimited, another spreadsheet format, or a multitude of other file types as shown in the drop-down menu from the "Save as type" window. Use caution when saving as non-Excel file formats since many of the features of Excel are not data features that can be saved into these formats. Thus, when saved as a text or document file, the formatting and tables within the file will be lost.

When the save command is used it resets the Undo command. That is, if you conducted an event that could be reversed through the Undo (addressed elsewhere in the booklet) that ability will generally be lost when you save the worksheet.

EXERCISES

Exercise E2-2 (File 2e-2) Journalize transactions.

Selected transactions for Feng Shui, Inc., an interior decorating firm, in its first month of business are as follows:
1. Invested $16,000 cash in business in exchange for common stock.
2. Purchased used car for $6,500 cash for use in business.
3. Purchased supplies on account for $900.
4. Billed customers $2,500 for services performed.
5. Paid $300 cash for advertising start of business.
6. Received $1,200 cash from customers billed in (4) above.
7. Paid creditor $500 cash on account.
8. Declared and paid a $1,000 cash dividend.

Instructions:
Journalize the transactions using journal page J1 as a reference.

Exercise E2-4 (File 2e-4) Journalize transactions.

Presented below is information related to Monterey Real Estate Agency, Inc.:
Oct 1   Kelly Monterey begins business as a real estate agent with a cash investment of $15,000 in exchange for common stock.
Oct 2   Hires an administrative assistant.
Oct 3   Buys office furniture for $2,650 on account.
Oct 6   Sells a house and lot for R. Edwards; revenue due from Edwards $8,400 (not paid by Edwards at this time).
Oct 10   Receives cash of $200 as fees for renting an apartment for the owner.
Oct 27   Pays $1,800 on the balance indicated in the transaction of October 3.
Oct 30   Pays the administrative assistant $1,500 in salary for October.

Instructions:
Journalize the transactions for Monterey Real Estate Agency, Inc.

Exercise E2-8 (File 2e-8) Prepare journal entries and post using standard account form.

Selected transactions for Jane M. Huber Corporation during its first month of business are presented below:

Sept 1   Invested $40,000 cash in the business in exchange for common stock.
Sept 5   Purchased equipment for $18,000 paying $7,000 in cash and the balance on account.
Sept 25 Paid $4,000 cash on balance owed for equipment.
Sept 30 Declared and paid a $1,200 cash dividend.

Huber's chart of accounts shows:

No. 101 – Cash   No. – 201 – Accounts payable
No. 157 – Equipment   No. 311 – Common stock
                                No. 332 – Cash dividends.

Instructions:
(a) Journalize the transactions on page J1 of the journal (omit explanations).
(b) Post the transactions using the standard account form.

PROBLEMS

Problem P2-1A (File 2p-1a) Journalize a series of transactions.

Evergreen Park Corp. was started on April 1 by Susan and Bill Helms. The following selected events and transactions occurred during April:

Apr 1   Invested $100,000 cash in the business in exchange for common stock.
Apr 4   Purchased land costing $35,000 for cash.
Apr 8   Incurred advertising expense of $2,100 on account.
Apr 11 Paid salaries to employees $1,200.
Apr 12 Hired park manager at a salary of $4,500 per month, effective May 1.
Apr 13 Paid $1,800 for a one-year insurance policy.
Apr 17 Declared and paid a $900 cash dividend.
Apr 20 Received $7,200 in cash for admission fees.
Apr 25 Sold 100 coupon books for $30 each. Each book contains 6 coupons that entitle the holder to one admission to the park.
Apr 30 Received $6,200 in cash admissions fees.
Apr 30 Paid $900 on account for advertising incurred on April 8.

Evergreen uses the following accounts:

Cash   Accounts payable
Prepaid insurance   Unearned admissions
Land   Common stock
Dividends   Admissions revenue
Advertising expense
Salaries expense.

Instructions:
Journalize the April transactions.

Problem P2-3A (File 2p-3a) Journalize transactions, post, and prepare a trial balance.

JarJar Theater Inc. opens on April 1. All facilities were completed on March 31. At this time, the ledger showed:

No. 101 – Cash	$10,000	No. 201 – Accounts payable	$2,000
No. 140 – Land	10,000	No. 275 – Mortgage payable	9,000
No. 145 – Buildings	8,000	No. 311 – Common stock	23,000
No. 157 – Equipment	6,000		

Account No. 145 – Buildings consists of concession stand, projection room, ticket booth, and screen.

During April, the following events and transactions occurred:
Apr 2   Paid film rental of $1,000 on first movie.
Apr 3   Ordered two additional films at $500 each.
Apr 9   Received $2,100 cash from admissions.
Apr 10 Made $3,000 payment on mortgage and $500 on accounts payable.
Apr 11 Hired Tim Rowe to operate concession stand. Tim Rowe to pay JarJar Thearter 16% of gross receipts payable monthly.
Apr 12 Paid advertising expenses $600.
Apr 20 Received one of the films ordered on April 3 and was billed $500. The film will be shown in April.
Apr 25 Received $4,600 cash from admissions.
Apr 29 Paid salaries $1,900.
Apr 30 Received statement from Tim Rowe showing gross receipts of $1,500 and the balance due to JarJar Theater of $170 for April. Tim Rowe paid one-half of the balance due and will remit the remainder on May 5.
Apr 30 Prepaid $800 rental on special film to be run in May.

In addition to the accounts identified above, the chart of accounts shows:

No. 112 – Accounts receivable	No. 610 – Advertising expense
No. 136 – Prepaid rentals	No. 632 – Film rental expense
No. 405 – Admission revenue	No. 726 – Salaries expense
No. 406 – Concession revenue	

Instructions:
(a) Enter the beginning balances in the ledger as of April 1. Insert a check mark in the reference column of the ledger for the beginning balance.
(b) Journalize the April transactions.
(c) Post the April journal entries to the ledger. Assume that all entries are posted from page 1 of the journal.
(d) Prepare a trial balance on April 30, 2002.

Problem P2-1B (File 2p-1b) Journalize a series of transactions.

The SurePar Miniature Golf and Driving Range Inc. was opened on March 1 by Mike Hatton. The following selected events and transactions occurred during March:

Mar 1   Invested $80,000 cash in the business in exchange for common stock.

Mar 3   Purchased Wabasha's Golf Land for $55,000 cash. The price consists of land - $28,000, building - $21,000, and equipment - $6,000. (Make one compound journal entry.)

Mar 5   Advertised the opening of the driving range and miniature golf course, paying advertising expenses of $1,500.

Mar 6   Paid cash $1,800 for a one-year insurance policy.

Mar 10 Purchased golf clubs and other equipment for $2,500 from T. Wood Company, payable in 30 days.

Mar 18 Received $1,200 in cash for golf fees earned.

Mar 19 Sold 100 coupon books for $20 each. Each book contains 10 coupons that enable the holder to one round of miniature golf or to hit one bucket of golf balls.

Mar 25 Declared and paid a $700 cash dividend.

Mar 30 Paid salaries of $900.

Mar 30 Paid T. Woods Company in full.

Mar 31 Received $600 for golf fees earned.

The company uses the following accounts:

Cash	Unearned revenue
Prepaid insurance	Common stock
Land	Dividends
Buildings	Golf revenue
Equipment	Advertising expense
Accounts payable	Salaries expense

Instructions:
Journalize the March transactions.

Problem P2-3B (File 2p-3b) Journalize transactions, post, and prepare a trial balance

The Mariner Theater Corp. owned by John Enright, will begin operations in March. The Mariner will be unique in that it will show only triple or quadruple features of sequential theme movies. As of February 28, the ledger of Mariner showed:

No. 101 – Cash	$20,000	No. 157 – Equipment	$16,000
No. 140 – Land	42,000	No. 201 – Accounts payable	16,000
No. 145 – Buildings	18,000	No. 311 – Common stock	23,000

During the month of March the following events and transactions occurred:

Mar 2   Acquired the four *Star Wars* movies (Star Wars – A New Hope, The Empire Strikes Back, The Return of the Jedi, and The Phantom Menace) to be shown for the first three weeks of March. The film rental was $20,000; $4,000 was paid in cash and $16,000 will be paid on March 10th.

Mar 3   Ordered the four *Star Trek* movies to be shown the last 10 days of March. They will cost

$500 per night.

Mar 9   Received $7,500 cash from admissions.

Mar 10 Paid balance due on *Star Wars* movies rental and $3,000 on February 28 accounts payable.

Mar 11 Hired Holly Littlefield to operate concession stand. Littlefield is to pay Mariner Theater 15% of gross receipts payable monthly.

Mar 12 Paid advertising expenses of $750.

Mar 20 Received $6,800 cash from admissions.

Mar 20 Received the *Star Trek* movies and paid the rental fee of $5,000.

Mar 31 Paid salaries of $4,800.

Mar 31 Received statement from Holly Littlefield showing gross receipts from concessions of $12,000 and the balance due to Mariner Theater of $1,800 for March. Littlefield paid one-half the balance due and will remit the remainder on April 5.

Mar 31 Received $14,500 cash from admissions.

In addition to the accounts identified above, the chart of accounts includes:

No. 112 – Accounts receivable	No. 610 – Advertising expense
No. 405 – Admission revenue	No. 632 – Film rental expense
No. 406 – Concession revenue	No. 726 – Salaries expense

Instructions:

(a) Enter the beginning balances in the ledger. Insert a check mark in the reference column of the ledger for the beginning balance.

(b) Journalize the March transactions.

(c) Post the March journal entries to the ledger. Assume that all entries are posted from page 1 of the journal.

(d) Prepare a trial balance on March 31, 2002.

CHAPTER 3

ADJUSTING THE ACCOUNTS

CHAPTER OUTLINE

CLUES, HINTS, AND TIPS

Sum formula

The Sum formula of Excel is an easily understood tool. When the entry of data into a cell starts as "=SUM(" Excel is looking for a math function to follow. You can enter basic data as "=SUM(2+3+4)" and Excel will calculate the answer as 9. You can also reference cells such as the formula in cell J43 of the Demo file. This cell contains the formula "=SUM(I41-J42)". This formula subtracts the value in Cell I41 ($50,000) from the value in Cell J42 ($40,000) to calculate the amount of capital paid-in in excess of par value for common stock for the entry. You must determine the appropriate formula to place into the cell and the appropriate references. The transaction states that the owner initiated business by buying 40,000 shares of $1 par common stock with $50,000 cash. The formula in Cell I41 is a "Look-to" formula addressed earlier in the booklet. It simply references the Cell D16 which contains the cash contributed. In Cell J42 the formula determines the amount to be credited to common stock by multiplying the number of shares, a value contained in Cell D14, by the par value of the shares, a value contained in Cell D15. The result of this mathematical operation is $40,000. These two values are the independent values of the formula contained in Cell J43. Since you determined and placed the amount of cash contributed to the company in Cell I41 and you determined the value of the capital stock issued in the transaction in Cell J42, the difference, the amount going to Capital paid-in in excess of par value for common stock is the result of subtracting the common stock value from the cash. This action is the action of the formula does in Cell J43.

With the "=SUM(" you must contain the formula with parenthesis marking the beginning and end of the formula run. You can also use parenthesis to contain and isolate the math operations precedent within Excel. Excel will do operations of multiplication and division before operations of addition and subtraction. Therefore the formula =sum(3*4+1) will result in 13, 3 multiplied by 4 and then 1 added to the result of the multiplication operation. If you had wanted to multiple the sum of 4+1 by 3 the formula could be written as =sum(4+1)*3 or =sum((4+1)*3). The use of multiple parentheses is common and accepted within Excel as it is in any other discipline of basic math operations.

If the formula is simple you can shorten the sum formula to =3+4+5 and the result will be 12. If Excel can understand the basic formula the use of sum to start the formula is unnecessary.

Excel will also mix constants with cell references within the formula. For example, in Cell I73 of the Demo file is a formula that calculates the interest payable on the bank note. It takes the principle of the note, $250,000, a value contained in Cell D21, and multiplies it by the annual interest rate contained in Cell D22, a value of 10%. Since the bank note was only out for a 6-month period, the additional factor of 6/12 is added to the formula to recognize a 6 month period of a fiscal year. With this presentation of 6 months it is reinforced why the multiplier is there within the formula. This technique will also preclude entering a 4 month period as 0.25 vise 0.33 as can occasionally happen.

Excel starts all addition, subtraction, multiplication, and division formulas with "=". This lead-in is merely a trigger for Excel. If the sum function is used within an imbedded formula, the equal sign is not used. Imbedded formulas are shown in the general ledger balance columns. Examine Cell J127 to see an embedded formula. Embedded formulas are addressed later in the booklet.

Freeze panes

The freeze pane function is invoked on the demo file upon opening. This function splits the single worksheet into two or more separately displayed panes. This view is controlled through the path Window>Split. To invoke it, place your cursor on the row numbers at the left near the center of the display pane or into the "A" column. Then follow the path Window>Split from the menu bar. Excel will split the screen and provide a scroll bar for each pane. In this manner the data from the problem can be read in the upper pane while doing journal entries in the lower pane. To demonstrate a further enhancement of this function, set your upper pane to show rows 11 through 17 while showing rows 41 through 44 in the lower pane. You can recreate the journal entry by clicking into cell B41 of the lower pane and typing "=" (without the quotation marks), then click your cursor onto cell B11 of the upper pane. When you hit the enter key, tab, or click into another cell, the date of Jan 2 appears in the date cell of the journal entry. Saving you time and the risk of data error through typing. Since the account to be debited is cash, you can do one of several things, you can type Cash into the debit account title area or you can do another look-to formula for the account title in the general ledger. Examination of the general ledger will show that the Cash account title is contained in Cell B79 while the cash account number, used when posting, is in Cell J79. So try the formulas =B79 and =J79 in the appropriate cells.

This capability of split screens is handy and precludes excessive scrolling and losing your place while working within the templates. If you place your cursor nearer to the center of the display and invoke freeze panes or split screens, you may end up with 4 panes to deal with. In this case the control of the display areas is interactive between the left & right and upper & lower panes through the scroll bars. Becoming comfortable with the appearance and proficient with the use of freeze panes or split panes greatly reduces your time to accomplish the tasks and reduces scrolling.

Page setup

The presentation of Excel data is dependent on page setup and page break positioning. The access to page setup can be accomplished through the path File>Page Setup. The dialog box the pops up appears as:

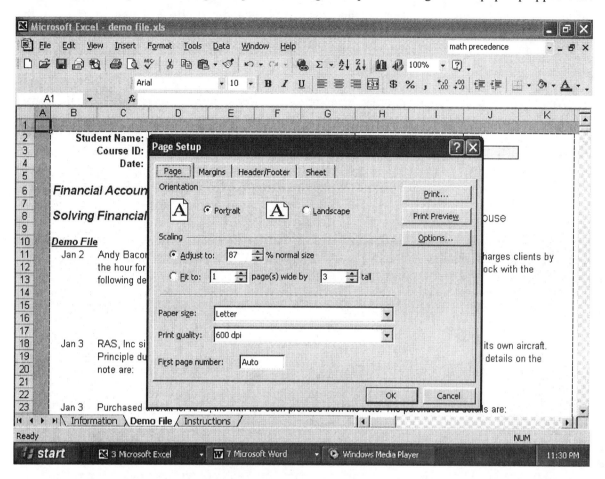

The page tab controls portrait or landscape view and the important function of "Fit to". With the "Fit to" capability you determine the pages that your Excel file will print by width and height. If you print a file only to find that one column of 8 is contained on a second sheet, consider telling Excel to print to 1 sheet wide. You can always over guess the pages needed without penalty. For example, if you have 4 columns of 1" wide each and 50 rows approximating 9' in height, you can instruct Excel to fit it to 10 pages wide and 20 pages tall and Excel will print the document on 1 single sheet. If you set the "Adjust to" selection to a value, Excel will obey that value. Taking your 4 columns, 50 rows and setting "Adjust to" to 500%, Excel will consume many sheets obeying your orders as the printed columns will be approximately 5" wide each (1" X 5 X 500%) resulting in total column width of 20 inches, and row heights of approximately 45" (9" X 500%). Excel will obey the last choice selected between the "Adjust to" and "Fit to" options. Only one can be invoked at a time. Print preview and then page break preview can be accessed from this tab as well.

The margins tab controls the upper, lower, left and right margins as well as placement upon the page. By selecting the center horizontally or vertically, the data can be centered on the page for a very nice presentation if appropriate. Seldom is financial data such as journals and ledgers centered both vertically and horizontally.

The header/footer tab allows you to place header and/or footer information on each printed sheet. This capability is on each of the templates. The template data shows the file name, the tab, the page of pages, the date and time. This has been included so that the compilation of multiple papers is easier. Click onto the header/footer and click on Custom Footer. The data contained within the footer will be shown. Holding your cursor over any of the numerous icons for several moments will reveal that icon's function. There are numerous default headers and footers that can be utilized through the drop-down menus.

The sheet tab contains numerous data bits that are very useful and versatile. The first bit of data is the established print area of the worksheet in the top data window. With the demo file this is B2:K176, or in English, the print area starts at Cell B2 and contains all of the cells down to row 176 and all the way to the right to include column K. This tab also controls whether a specific row or set of rows will appear at the top of every sheet printed and if a specific column or set of columns will be printed at the left of each page printed. Assume that you are printing inventory reports running 125 pages. They contain part number, location code, description, quantity on hand, quantity on order, quantity in WIP, and value. By placing the titles row on each sheet through this function, you will retain column identity without building it into the worksheet. This transposes to columns to identify rows as well. You may invoke columns and rows at the same time. Also on this tab you can select the order in which the pages will print. If you are printing data that is presented by rows and its taking four sheets wide, you may want to print the across and then down so that the first four sheets address the rows contained before introducing the second set of rows. Gridlines on or off are controlled on this tab. Many people do not like grid lines on their data. The templates have them turned off but this tab can change that for the individual template. This does not control the grid line presentation on the display. The grid line on the screen is controlled by the path Tools>Options>View. If viewed through that path, they will not print. Neither of these options affects cells that have borders placed on them.

Page break preview

Page break preview is found through the path View>Page Break Preview from the menu bar or from a button on sheet preview. Sheet preview is the white sheet with the folded corner and magnifying glass on the task bar. Page break preview will show how the pages are going to print with the current printer and page settings. The page breaks can be moved and repositioned from within this view. Hint – When resetting page breaks start in the upper left corner and work down and to the right. Starting at the bottom may result in too much on page 1 or too little. To close page break preview you follow the path View>Normal. Page break preview is dependent upon page setup and printer functions. Most printers can print to within ½" of each edge of an 8 ½ X 11" sheet of paper. There are a few printers that require larger margins. The templates have been designed to provide the largest application usage so the standards of 1" margins are seldom violated.

EXERCISES

Exercise E3-3 (File 3e-3) Prepare adjusting entries from selected account data.

The ledger of Easy Rental Agency on March 31 of the current year includes the following selected accounts before adjusting entries have been prepared:

	Debit	Credit
Prepaid insurance	$3,600	
Supplies	2,800	
Equipment	25,000	

Accumulated depreciation – Equipment		$8,400
Notes payable		20,000
Unearned rent		9,900
Rent revenue		60,000
Interest expense		
Wages expense	14,000	

An analysis of the accounts shows the following:
1. The equipment depreciates $250 per month.
2. One-third of the unearned rent was earned during the quarter.
3. Interest of $500 is accrued on the notes payable.
4. Supplies on hand total $650.
5. Insurance expires at the rate of $300 per month.

Instructions:
Prepare the adjusting entries at March 31, assuming that adjusting entries are made quarterly. Additional accounts are: Depreciation expense, Insurance expense, Interest payable, and Supplies expense.

Exercise E3-5 (File 3e-5) Prepare adjusting entries.
The trial balance of Pioneer Advertising Agency Inc. is shown below:

PIONEER ADVERTISING AGENCY INC.
Trial Balance
October 31, 2002

	Debit	Credit
Cash	$15,200	
Advertising supplies	2,500	
Prepaid insurance	600	
Office equipment	5,000	
Notes payable		$5,000
Accounts payable		2,500
Unearned revenue		1,200
Common stock		10,000
Retained earnings		0
Dividends	500	
Service revenue		10,000
Salaries expense	4,000	
Rent expense	900	
	$28,700	$28,700

In lieu of the adjusting entries shown in the text book at October 31, assume the following adjustment data:
1. Advertising supplies on hand at October 31 total $1,100.
2. Expired insurance for the month is $100.
3. Depreciation for the month is $50.
4. Unearned revenue for October totals $600.
5. Services provided but unbilled at October 31 is $300.
6. Interest accrued at October 31 is $70.
7. Accrued salaries at October 31 are $1,400.

Instructions:
Prepare the adjusting entries for the items above.

Exercise E3-12 (File 3e-12) Journalize transactions and adjusting entries using appendix.

At Devereaux Company, prepayments are debited to expense when paid, and unearned revenues are credited to revenue when received. During January of the current year, the following transactions occurred:

Jan 2   Paid $1,800 for fire insurance protection for the year.
Jan 10 Paid $1,700 for supplies.
Jan 15 Received $5,100 for services to be performed in the future.

On January 31, it is determined that $1,500 of the services fees have been earned and that there are $800 in supplies.

Instructions:
(a) Journalize and post the January transactions. (Use T accounts.)
(b) Journalize and post the adjusting entries at January 31.
(c) Determine the ending balances in each of the accounts.

PROBLEMS

Problem P3-2A (File 3p-2a) Prepare adjusting entries, adjusted trial balance, and financial statements.

Muddy River Resort Inc. opened for business on June 1 with eight air-conditioned units. Its trial balance before adjustment on August 31 is as follows:

MUDDY RIVER RESORT INC.
Trial Balance
August 31, 2002

Acct Nbr:	Acct Title	Debit	Credit
101	Cash	$19,600	
126	Supplies	3,300	
130	Prepaid insurance	6,000	
140	Land	25,000	
143	Cottages	125,000	
149	Furniture	26,000	
201	Accounts payable		$6,500
208	Unearned rent		7,400
275	Mortgage payable		80,000
311	Common stock		100,000
332	Dividends	5,000	
429	Rent revenue		80,000
622	Repair expense	3,600	

726	Salaries expense	51,000	
732	Utilities expense	9,400	
		$273,900	$273,900

In addition to those accounts listed on the trial balance, the chart of accounts for Muddy River Resort Inc. also contains the following accounts and account numbers:

Acct Nbr:	Account title:
112	Accounts receivable
144	Accumulated depreciation – Cottages
150	Accumulated depreciation – Furniture
212	Salaries payable
230	Interest payable
620	Depreciation expense – Cottages
621	Depreciation expense – Furniture
631	Supplies expense
718	Interest expense
722	Insurance expense

Other data:
1. Insurance expires at the rate of $400 per month.
2. A count on August 31 shows $900 of supplies on hand.
3. Annual depreciation is $4,800 on cottages and $2,400 on furniture.
4. Unearned rent of $5,100 was earned prior to August 31.
5. Salaries of $400 were unpaid at August 31.
6. Rentals of $800 were due from tenants at August 31. (Use accounts receivable.)
7. The mortgage interest rate is 12% per year. (The mortgage was taken out on August 1st.)

Instructions:
(a) Journalize the adjusting entries on August 31 for the 3-month period June 1~August 31.
(b) Prepare a ledger using the three-column form of account. Enter the trial balance amounts and post the adjusting entries. (Use J1 as the posting reference.)
(c) Prepare an adjusted trial balance on August 31.
(d) Prepare an income statement and a retained earnings statement for the 3 months ending August 31 and a balance sheet as of August 31.

Problem P3-5A (File 3p-5a) Journalize transactions and follow through accounting cycle to preparation of financial statements.

On September 1, 2002, the account balances of Rijo Equipment Repair Corp. were as follows:

Acct Nbr:	Account:	Debits:	Acct Nbr:	Account:	Credits:
101	Cash	$4,880	154	Accumulated depreciation	$1,500
112	Accounts receivable	3,520	201	Accounts payable	3,400
126	Supplies	2,000	209	Unearned service revenue	1,400
153	Store equipment	15,000	212	Salaries payable	500
			311	Common stock	10,000
			320	Retained earnings	8,600
		$25,400			$25,400

During September the following summary transactions were completed:

Sept 8   Paid $1,100 for salaries due employees, of which $600 is for September.

Sept 10 Received $1,200 cash from customers on account.

Sept 12 Received $3,400 cash for services performed in September.

Sept 15 Purchased store equipment on account $3,000.

Sept 17 Purchased supplies on account $1,500.

Sept 20 Paid creditors $4,500 on account.

Sept 22 Paid September rent $500.

Sept 25 Paid salaries $1,050.

Sept 27 Performed services on account and billed customers for services rendered $700.

Sept 29 Received $650 from customers for future services.

Adjusting data consists of:
1. Supplies on hand of $1,700.
2. Accrued salaries payable $400.
3. Depreciation is $200 per month.
4. Unearned service revenue of $1,450 is earned.

Instructions:

(a) Enter the September 1 balances into ledger accounts.

(b) Journalize the September transactions.

(c) Post to the ledger accounts. Use J1 for the posting reference. Use the following accounts:

Acct Nbr:	Acct Title:
407	Service revenue
615	Depreciation expense
631	Supplies expense
726	Salaries expense
729	Rent expense

(d) Prepare a trial balance at September 30.

(e) Journalize and post adjusting entries.

(f) Prepare an adjusted trial balance.

(g) Prepare an income statement and a retained earnings statement for September and a balance sheet for September 30.

Problem P3-1B (File 3p-1b) Prepare adjusting entries, post to ledger accounts, and prepare an adjusted trial balance.

Julie Brown started her own consulting firm, Astromech Consulting, on May 1, 2002. The trial balance at May 31 is as follows:

ASTROMECH CONSULTING
Trial Balance
May 31, 2002

Acct Nbr:	Acct title:	Debit:	Credit:
101	Cash	$6,500	
110	Accounts receivable	4,000	
120	Prepaid insurance	3,600	
130	Supplies	1,500	

135	Office furniture	12,000	
200	Accounts payable		$3,500
230	Unearned service revenue		3,000
311	Common stock		19,100
400	Service revenue		6,000
510	Salaries expense	3,000	
520	Rent expense	1,000	
		$31,600	$31,600

In addition to those accounts listed on the trial balance, the chart of accounts for Astromech Consulting also contains the following accounts and account numbers:

Acct Nbr:	Acct Title:
136	Accumulated depreciation – Office furniture
210	Travel payable
220	Salaries payable
530	Depreciation expense
540	Insurance expense
550	Travel expense
560	Supplies expense

Other data:
1. $500 of supplies have been used during the month.
2. Travel expense incurred but not paid on May 31, 2002, $200.
3. The insurance policy is for 2 years.
4. $1,000 of the balance in the unearned service revenue account remains unearned at the end of the month.
5. May 31 is a Wednesday, and employees are paid on Fridays. Astromech Consulting has two employees, who are paid $500 each for a 5-day work week.
6. The office furniture has a 5-year life with no salvage value. It is being depreciated at $20 per month for 60 months.
7. Invoices representing $2,000 of services performed during the month have not been recorded as of May 31.

Instructions:
(a) Prepare the adjusting entries for the month of May. Use J4 as the page number for your journal.
(b) Post the adjusting entries to the ledger accounts. Enter the totals from the trial balance as beginning account balances and place a check mark in the posting reference column.
(c) Prepare an adjusted trial balance at May 31, 2002.

Problem P3-5B (File 3p-5b) Journalize transactions and follow through accounting cycle to preparation of financial statements.

On November 1, 2002, the account balances of Thao Equipment Repair Corp. were as follows:

Acct Nbr:	Account:	Debits:	Acct Nbr:	Account:	Credits:
101	Cash	$2,790	154	Accumulated depreciation	$500
112	Accounts receivable	2,510	201	Accounts payable	2,100
126	Supplies	2,000	209	Unearned service revenue	1,400
153	Store equipment	10,000	212	Salaries payable	500

	311	Common stock	10,000
	320	Retained earnings	2,800
$17,300			$17,300

During November the following summary transactions were completed:

Nov 8   Paid $1,100 for salaries due employees, of which $600 is for November.

Nov 10 Received $1,200 cash from customers on account.

Nov 12 Received $1,400 cash for services performed in November.

Nov 15 Purchased store equipment on account $3,000.

Nov 17 Purchased supplies on account $1,500.

Nov 20 Paid creditors on account $2,500.

Nov 22 Paid November rent $300.

Nov 25 Paid salaries $1,000.

Nov 27 Performed services on account and billed customers for services rendered $900.

Nov 29 Received $550 from customers for future services.

Adjusting data consists of:
1. Supplies on hand of $1,600.
2. Accrued salaries payable $500.
3. Depreciation is $120 per month.
4. Unearned service revenue of $1,250 is earned.

Instructions:
(a) Enter the November 1 balances into ledger accounts.
(b) Journalize the November transactions.
(c) Post to the ledger accounts. Use J1 for the posting reference. Use the following accounts:

Acct Nbr:	Account title:
407	Service revenue
615	Depreciation expense
631	Supplies expense
726	Salaries expense
729	Rent expense

(d) Prepare a trial balance at November 30.
(e) Journalize and post adjusting entries.
(f) Prepare an adjusted trial balance.
(g) Prepare an income statement and a retained earnings statement for November and a balance sheet for November 30.

CHAPTER 4

COMPLETION OF THE ACCOUNTING CYCLE

CHAPTER OUTLINE

Clues, Hints, and Tips
  Print area
  Print Preview
  Printing
Exercises
  Exercise E4-5 (File 4e-5) Derive adjusting entries
    from worksheet data
  Exercise E4-11 (File 4e-11) Prepare closing and
    and reversing entries
Problems
  Problem P4-3A (File 4p-3a) Prepare financial

statements, closing entries, and post-closing
trial balance.
Problem P4-5A (File 4p-5a) Complete all steps
  in accounting cycle
Problem P4-1B (File 4p-1b) Prepare a worksheet,
  financial statements, and adjusting and closing
  entries
Problem P4-4B (File 4p-4b) Complete worksheet,
  prepare classified balance sheet, entries, and
  post-closing trial balance

CLUES, HINTS, AND TIPS

Print Area

As addressed previously, Excel can and will consume as much paper as needed to print a worksheet. Sometimes this is not necessary. For example, you have constructed a worksheet presenting data and the actual data presentation is only one physical page. However, to clarify your calculations and work, you have numerous areas elsewhere on the worksheet with extensive detail and support material. If not provided with parameters for printing, Excel will print in an 8 ½ X 11" format for standard bond paper every cell that has been touched by a calculation or used as a reference for the worksheet. With this example, all of your supporting calculations are going to be printed and the printing will normally be in a vertical then left to right format in portrait mode.

This is easily handled within Excel. The demo file has a predefined print area to preclude this and can be used as an example. On the Demo File tab of the demo file, you will notice that the worksheet is outlined by a gray border. This border has no function with the print area, it is merely provided as a visual reference of the print area by the author. Anything you enter inside the gray border will be printed on the sheet. Any item on or outside the border will not be printed on the worksheet printout. To examine the worksheet's predefined printed area follow the path File>Page setup>Sheet and read the values contained in the upper window of the Print area tab. If you know the print area you want, you can enter it directly into the print area window on the Sheet tab by using cell references and separating them by a colon. However, you can also define the print area from the worksheet itself. To demonstrate this, click into and make cell B2 of the demo file the active cell. When this is done the cell will have a heavy border around it. Now, press and hold the left mouse button down, while holding the left mouse button down, sweep the mouse cursor down and to the right to highlight all of the cells within the gray borders. Once the cells are highlighted, release the mouse button and *do not* click back onto the worksheet or your highlight will be lost. Follow the path File>Print area>Set print area and click on the Set print area selection. Now you have defined the print area with only one cell reference required – B2, and that was only required to tell you where to start. You could have just as easily clicked into the upper, leftmost cell and highlighted down and right.

You can also print areas that are not adjacent to each other. For example, assume that you want to print the range from B2 through L50, and the range from R55 through Q90. Open up the sheet tab, click into the set print area window, click into Cell B2 and highlight through Cell L50, then click into Cell R55 and highlight through Q90 and click OK. Excel will identify these two ranges in the window separated by a comma. You can define multiple ranges this way. Remember that after highlighting and identifying the first area, you must use the scroll bars to move to the second area. Moving the cursor through the arrow keys will include those cells in the print.

You cannot define one sheet to be printed portrait and another landscape within Excel. Your solution to that is an external vendor package or simply have look to formulas on another worksheet and having that worksheet setup with portrait or landscape as desired. It is best if you always preview the worksheet before printing to avoid paper consumption. And, once printed, review the document to insure that it is correct.

Print Preview

By clicking on the icon on the task bar of white sheet of page with the upper right corner turned over and a magnifying glass overlaying it you will access the print preview of your document. If there is more than one page there will be a scroll bar on the right side of the screen. If the print preview presentation fills the page chances are you are in the Zoom mode. Simply click on the sheet or on ZOOM on the menu bar and you should be presented with an overall picture of your document.

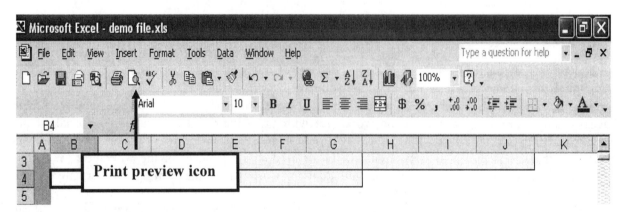

From this screen you will see how the how the document will appear in its printed mode. This includes features such as headers and footers as well as margins. You can also adjust the page in this presentation. By clicking on the Margins button in the menu bar at the top you will be given presentation of present placement of the margins and columns. You can adjust the margins and column widths at this point by placing the mouse cursor on the margin or column marker and pressing and holding the left mouse button down. While the mouse button is being held down, drag the cursor left, right, up or down, as desired. The margins at the outer areas of the sheet at the top and bottom of the sheet are those of the page and are defaulted to the values found under the path File>Page setup>Margins. These margins are fully adjustable but will always be at or outside of the file margins. The area between the page margins and the file margins is where the headers and footers are placed at the top and bottom. The margins at the side of the sheet are those of the page and the file unless you have a page narrower than the file page. In that case the file will be oriented into the upper right corner of the page.

There are numerous changes you can make within print preview besides margins and column width. By clicking on the Page setup button you can adjust almost every item accessible through File>Page setup except the print area. This must be set from the normal view mode or from the page break view mode. Remember that under the Margins tab within page setup you can center your page horizontally, vertically, or both if you desire.

Printing

Excel will print from several different commands and paths. The quickest while using the templates is the print icon on the task bar. This symbol is the printer. By clicking on this icon Excel and Microsoft Windows will print the currently active document through the default printer as established by the Windows setup under printers. When printing other worksheets this command may result in excessive paper being used in the printing process. The difference is that the Excel templates accompanying this booklet already have predefined layouts and paper breaks. For original worksheets the layout and print area should be verified and adjusted as described in the above sections.

If you do not desire the Windows default printer you can follow the path File>Print and a dialog box will appear as shown below:

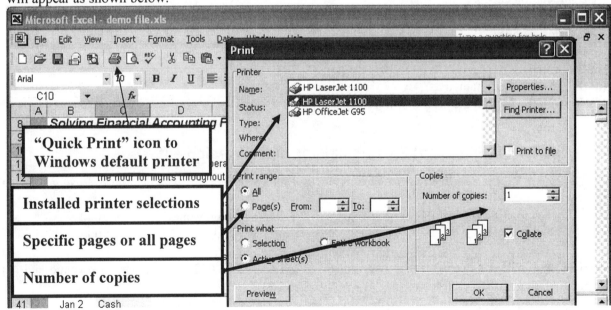

From this dialog box you can select printers installed on the desktop system, on the network or fax drivers that may be installed. If your worksheet consists of multiple pages, you can select any relevant range. For example, if your worksheet consists of 5 pages, you can select All to get pages 1 through 5, select from page 2 to 4, select from 3 to 3 or elect to print only the highlighted or selected area through the selection within the Print what box below the Print range box. You can also determine the number of copies desired and whether those copies are collated or not. The default is to collate multiple prints. This may not be desired if presenting a large amount of information to a group as they may become involved in scanning the depths of the document during your presentation. By not collating the documents, you can pass single sheets out, containing exposure without have to resort the document. After all selections are made printing is initiated by clicking OK. Excel and Windows will normally print the document to the selected printer without further action.

EXERCISES

Exercise E4-5 (File 4e-5) Derive adjusting entries from worksheet data

Selected worksheet data for Karen Allman Company are presented below:

Account titles:	Trial balance:		Adjusted trial balance	
	Debit	Credit	Debit	Credit
Accounts receivable	?		34,000	
Prepaid insurance	26,000		18,000	
Supplies	9,000		?	
Accumulated depreciation		12,000		?
Salaries expense		?		6,000
Service revenue		88,000		95,000
Insurance expense			?	
Depreciation expense			10,000	
Supplies expense			4,000	
Salaries expense	?		49,000	

Instructions:
(a) Fill in the missing amounts.
(b) Prepare the adjusting entries that were made.

Exercise E4-11 (File 4e-11) Prepare closing and reversing entries

On December 31, the adjusted trial balance of Becky Employment Agency shows the following selected data:

Accounts receivable	$24,000	Commission revenue	$92,000
Interest expense	7,800	Interest payable	2,000

Analysis shows that adjusting entries were made to (1) accrue $5,000 of commission revenue and (2) accrue $2,000 interest expense.

Instructions:
(a) Prepare the closing entries for the temporary accounts at December 31.
(b) Prepare the reversing entries on January 1.
(c) Post the entries in (a) and (b). Rule and balance the accounts. (Use T accounts.)

(d) Prepare the entries to record (1) the collection of the accrued commissions on January 10 and (2) the payment of all interest due ($2,700) on January 15.

(e) Post the entries in (d) to the temporary accounts.

PROBLEMS

Problem P4-3A (File 4p-3a) Prepare financial statements, closing entries, and post-closing trial balance.

The completed financial statement columns of the worksheet for Panaka Company are shown below:

PANAKA COMPANY
Worksheet
For the Year Ended December 31, 2002

Acct Nbr:	Account title:	Income Statement Debit:	Income Statement Credit:	Balance Sheet Debit:	Balance Sheet Credit:
101	Cash			10,200	
112	Accounts receivable			7,500	
130	Prepaid insurance			1,800	
157	Equipment			28,000	
167	Accumulated depreciation				8,600
201	Accounts payable				12,000
212	Salaries payable				3,000
311	Common stock				20,000
320	Retained earnings				14,000
332	Dividends			7,200	
400	Service revenue		44,000		
622	Repair expense	3,200			
711	Depreciation expense	2,800			
722	Insurance expense	1,200			
726	Salaries expense	36,000			
732	Utilities expense	3,700			
	Totals	46,900	44,000	54,700	57,600
	Net loss		2,900	2,900	
	Totals	46,900	46,900	57,600	57,600

Instructions:

(a) Prepare an income statement, a retained earnings statement, and a classified balance sheet. Stockholders made additional purchases of common stock of $4,000 during 2002.

(b) Prepare the closing entries.

(c) Post the closing entries and rule and balance the accounts. Use T accounts. The income summary account is account number 350.

(d) Prepare a post-closing trial balance.

Problem P4-5A (File 4p-5a) Complete all steps in accounting cycle

Ewok-Ackbar opened Ewok's Carpet Cleaners Inc. on March 1. During March, the following transactions were completed:

Mar 1   Issued $10,000 of common stock for $10,000 cash.
Mar 1   Purchased used truck for $6,000, paying $4,000 cash and the balance on account.
Mar 3   Purchased cleaning supplies for $1,200 on account.
Mar 5   Paid $1,800 cash on one-year insurance policy effective March 1.
Mar 14 Billed customers $2,800 for cleaning services.
Mar 18 Paid $1,500 cash on amount owed on truck and $500 on amount owed on cleaning supplies.
Mar 20 Paid $1,500 cash for employee salaries.
Mar 21 Collected $1,600 cash from customers billed on March 14th.
Mar 28 Billed customers $2,500 for cleaning services.
Mar 31 Paid gas and oil for month on truck, $200.
Mar 31 Declared and paid a $700 cash dividend.

The chart of accounts for Ewok's Carpet Cleaners Inc. contains the following accounts:

Acct Nbr:	Account title:	Acct Nbr:	Account title:
101	Cash	320	Retained earnings
112	Accounts receivable	350	Income summary
128	Cleaning supplies	400	Service revenue
130	Prepaid insurance	633	Gas & oil expense
157	Equipment	634	Cleaning supplies expense
158	Accumulated depreciation-Equipment	711	Depreciation expense
201	Accounts payable	722	Insurance expense
212	Salaries payable	726	Salaries expense
311	Common stock		

Instructions:

(a) Journalize and post the March transactions. Use page J1 for the journal and the thee-column form of account.
(b) Prepare a trial balance at March 31 on a worksheet.
(c) Enter the following adjustments on the work sheet and complete the work sheet:
   (1) Earned but unbilled revenue at March 31 was $600.
   (2) Depreciation on equipment for the month was $250.
   (3) One-twelfth of the insurance expired.
   (4) An inventory count shows $400 of cleaning supplies on hand at March 31.
   (5) Accrued but unpaid employees salaries were $500.
(d) Journalize and post adjusting entries. Use page J2 for the journal.
(e) Prepare the income statement and a statement of retained earnings for March and a classified balance sheet for March 31.
(f) Journalize and post closing entries and complete the closing process. Use page J3 for the journal.
(g) Prepare a post-closing trial balance at March 31.

Problem P4-1B (File 4p-1b) Prepare a work sheet, financial statements, and adjusting and closing entries

The trial balance columns of the work sheet for Phantom Roofing Inc. at March 31, 2002, are as follows:

PHANTOM ROOFING INC.

Work Sheet

For the Month Ended March 31, 2002

	Trial balance	
Account titles	Debit	Credit
Cash	2,500	
Accounts receivable	1,600	
Roofing supplies	1,100	
Equipment	6,000	
Accumulated depreciation-Equipment		1,200
Accounts payable		1,100
Unearned revenue		300
Common stock		5,000
Retained earnings		2,000
Dividends	600	
Service revenue		3,000
Salaries expense	700	
Miscellaneous expense	100	
	12,600	12,600

Other data:

(1) A physical count reveals only $220 of roofing supplies on hand.

(2) Depreciation for March is $200.

(3) Unearned revenue amounted to $200 after adjustment on March 31.

(4) Accrued salaries are $400.

Instructions:

(a) Enter the trial balance on a work sheet and complete the work sheet.

(b) Prepare an income statement and owner's equity statement for the month of March and a classified balance sheet at March 31. No additional issuances of stock occurred in March.

(c) Journalize the adjusting entries from the adjustments columns of the work sheet.

(d) Journalize the closing entries from the financial statement columns of the work sheet.

Problem P4-4B (File 4p-4b) Complete work sheet, prepare classified balance sheet, entries, and post-closing trial balance

Rebecca Sherrick Management Services Inc. began business on January 1, 2002, with a capital investment of $120,000. The company manages condominiums for owners (Service revenue) and rents space in its own building (Rent revenue). The trial balance and adjusted trial balance columns of the work sheet at the end of the first year are as follows:

REBECCA SHERRICK MANAGEMENT SERVICES INC.
Work Sheet
For the Year Ended December 31, 2002

Account titles	Trial balance Debit	Trial balance Credit	Adjusted trial balance Debit	Adjusted trial balance Credit
Cash	$14,500		$14,500	
Accounts receivable	23,600		23,600	
Prepaid insurance	3,100		1,600	
Land	56,000		56,000	
Building	106,000		106,000	
Equipment	48,000		48,000	
Accounts payable		$10,400		$10,400
Unearned rent revenue		5,000		1,800
Mortgage payable		100,000		100,000
Common stock		90,000		90,000
Retained earnings		30,000		30,000
Dividends	20,000		20,000	
Service revenue		75,600		75,600
Rent revenue		23,000		26,200
Salaries expense	30,000		30,000	
Advertising expense	17,000		17,000	
Utilities expense	15,800		15,800	
Totals	$334,000	$334,000		
Insurance expense			1,500	
Depreciation expense-Building			2,500	
Accumulated depreciation-Building				2,500
Depreciation expense-Building			3,900	
Accumulated depreciation-Equipment				3,900
Interest expense			10,000	
Interest payable				10,000
Totals			$350,400	$350,400

Instructions:
(a) Prepare a complete work sheet.
(b) Prepare a classified balance sheet. (*Note*: $10,000 of the mortgage payable is due for payment next year.)
(c) Journalize the adjusting entries.
(d) Journalize the closing entries.
(e) Prepare a post-closing trial balance.

CHAPTER 5

ACCOUNTING FOR MERCHANDISING OPERATIONS

CHAPTER OUTLINE

CLUES, HINTS, AND TIPS

Today and Now

Excel has two functions that will assist you in inserting dates and times. By utilizing the function "=+TODAY()" Excel will present the date in the current default value for the worksheet. On January 1, 2002, this function would return 01/01/02 if that was the default of the worksheet and no other default had been applied to the cell. If the cell had been formatted to MMM D, YYYY format under custom the function would return Jan 1, 2002. Once the function is put into a cell, that cell can be formatted to present the date in the desired format. This function does not present time correctly.

To present date and time via a function use the "=+NOW()" function. This function correctly inserts the current time as well as date. Like the Today function, it can be formatted to obtain the precise desired format for the date and time, date only, or time only if desired.

Formatting cells

Excel has several ways to format cells and the data within a cell. To format a single cell, click into the cell to make it the active cell. If the format is intended for a single range of cells, click into the upper left, upper right, bottom left, or bottom right cell and sweep the range with the left mouse button down, highlighting and selecting all of the cells in the range. Formatting can be applied to more than one cell or one range is holding the control key down while selecting the sequential cells or ranges. Formatting can also be applied to a single column by clicking on the column identifier, a single row by clicking on the row number, or on multiple columns or rows by clicking on the column or row and then sweeping to right, left, up, or down to highlight all the columns or rows.

Once the cell or cells are selected right click the highlighted cell or cells and Excel will present you with a pop-up dialog box with the formatting options available at the time. That dialog box appears below:

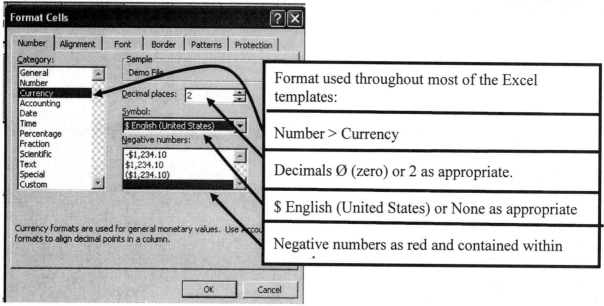

From this dialog box you can select any of the many formatting features available at the moment. If a feature is grayed out or faded, that feature is not available at the moment. For the Excel templates, the formatting is generally Currency with either Ø (zero) or 2 (two) as appropriate.

In selecting number formatting Excel positions the right hand number appropriate for the formatting selection. Provided below is a display of numerous Excel formats in positive and negative numbers. A close examination of this screen print will reveal that not all of the numbers are aligned in the same vertical plane at the right side of the column. This occurs when Excel is formatted to display negative numbers with a preceding "-" negative sign in some cells while other cells display negative numbers contained within parenthesis "()", Excel will position the numbers farther to the right if a preceding negative sign is used since the space is not needed to the right in the event of the closing parentheses. The solution for a ragged display of numbers that do not right align correctly is to check that the formatting of the numbers is all the same by selecting and highlighting the cells and right-clicking them followed by selecting the desired format even if it appears correct. Excel will occasionally only show the formatting of the upper left hand cell of a range or multiple selection.

1	Input value:	Format:
2	$ 123,456.79	Dollar sign on tool bar
3	$(123,456.79)	Dollar sign on tool bar
4	12345679%	Percentage sign on tool bar
5	-12345679%	Percentage sign on tool bar
6	123,456.79	Comma on tool bar
7	(123,456.79)	Comma on tool bar
8	123456.789	Format dialog box - Number - General
9	-123456.789	Format dialog box - Number - General
10	123,456.79	Format dialog box - Number - Number - 1000 separator, red () for negative, no sign, 2 decimal places
11	(123,456.79)	Format dialog box - Number - Number - 1000 separator, red () for negative, no sign, 2 decimal places
12	$123,456.79	Format dialog box - Number - Currency - Number - red () for negative, $ sign, 2 decimal places
13	($123,456.79)	Format dialog box - Number - Currency - Number - red () for negative, $ sign, 2 decimal places

The formatting dialog box also contains the alignment tab. From this tab you can align the contents of the cell in numerous horizontal and vertical formats as well as change its orientation and stack it. Through the orientation function you rotate your data through various angles. The insert below contains an orientation sample. By selecting the vertical mode occasionally referred to as "Hotel signage" referring to the letters H-O-T-E-L will be printed vertically on the sign in front of the establishment. This is also shown in the insert. Text wrap will try to keep the preset column width while creating a second, third, and fourth row presentation within the cell of long data. You can force this presentation by the keystrokes "Alt-Shift" instead of enter or space. In the insert Alt-Shift produces the same presentation as text wrap except that you control the break points of Alt-Shift whereas text wrap makes its own decisions.

The "Merge cells" command is also on the alignment tab. This function will create one cell that occupies two or row or columns or both. To utilize the merge cells function, click into the cell that you want to be the upper left most location and cell of the merged cell. Then, with the left mouse button held down, sweep right, down, or down and right highlighting and selecting the cells you want to be replaced by the new, larger, merged cell. When highlighted, right click the highlighted area, select format cells, select the alignment tab, and select merge cells. The highlights cells now become one single cell. Invoking the merge cells function will result the loss of all data but the data in the upper left most cell of the selection. If this function is invoked, it can be revoked by selecting the affected cell and then removing the check mark from the merged cells option.

The functions of font are as expected. You can change style, size, and color through this tab. It is on this tab that you will find super and sub script functions as well as strike through. You can also underline the text contained within a cell from this tab including single and double lines for accounting. However, if underlining is selected, it is only effective on cells with content in them, including spaces, and is only applicable to the cell. That is, if your entry covers two, three, or four columns, only the column or columns selected will be underlined and then, only if data actually appears within them.

The Borders tab allows you to place borders and intermediary lines to the highlighted cell or cells. You can put a thick line on the outer edges by selecting the heavier line first and then clicking the outline icon on the tab. You can then select a thinner line and place lines horizontally within the range. Excel will also allow you to place diagonal lines through a range. The functions available through this tab are directly associated with the cell or range selected at the moment. Excel will not allow you to place vertical or horizontal intermediary lines within a single cell through this cell, you can draw a line through the cell as explained later in the booklet.

Under the Patterns tab of the formatting dialog box you will find the colors to fill a cell and the available patterns for texture presentation of the colors. These functions were used on the templates to define the work area, outlined in gray, and the student focus areas, filled in yellow. To remove a color, simply select the cell or range, right click the selected cell or range, select format cells, select pattern and then select no color. This will remove both color and texture or pattern.

The last tab is the Protection tab. This tab allows you to invoke a minor level of protection on the worksheet or workbook. If you did not want another party to have the privilege of modifying your work sheet you can select the entire sheet by using the key strokes Ctrl-A or by clicking on the cell above the row 1 number and to the left of the column A letter, then right click the work sheet and select format cells. After selecting the protection tab select the Locked option. Ensure that the appearing checkmark is clear and distinct. If it is faded that indicates that the selected area contains more than one level of protection. Also on this tab is the Hidden option. If selected and activated any functions and formulas will be hidden from the viewer – that is, even if the cell contains a formula, the viewer will not see it in the formula window. Neither of these options are active until empowered by following the path Tools>Protection. From this point you can select protect workbook or worksheet as well as a couple of other options. When Protect a worksheet or Protect a workbook is selected you will be presented with a pop-up dialog box asking what privileges you want to grant the users and asking if a password will be utilized. You can leave the password blank if you desire. If a password is provided and later forgotten, you may not be able to recover the workbook or worksheet. As a matter of technique, if distributing a password protected workbook or worksheet, you may want to preserve an unprotected copy in a secure location. None of these protection levels is sophisticated and can be broken by an individual with intent. These levels of protection should not be relied upon to protect sensitive data.

Formatting within a cell

You can also invoke many of the formatting capabilities for cells onto and into the contents of a cell. For example, you want to entry into an Excel cell that the interest on the note payable is due on the 30th of each month. When the text is entered as "Interest on note payable is due on the 30th of each month" the text is not automatically superscripted. For this presentation highlight with the mouse the two characters "th" within the text, then right click the highlighted selection and select Format cells, then select superscript on the Font tab. Notice that not all of the tabs that appeared when Format cells was selected when the entire cell was selected now that you have only a portion of the text selected. Since the additional capabilities are not available, they were not presented, even grayed out or faded. Many of the formatting features can still be invoke upon the text within a cell.

EXERCISES

Exercise E5-7 (File 5e-7) Prepare multiple-step and single-step income statement

In its income statement for the year ended December 31, 2002, Berman Company reported the following condensed data:

Administrative expenses	$435,000	Selling expenses	$490,000
Cost of goods sold	1,289,000	Loss on sale of equipment	10,000
Interest expense	70,000	Net sales	2,350,000
Interest revenue	45,000		

Instructions:
(a) Prepare a multi-step income statement.
(b) Prepare a single-step income statement.

Exercise E5-10 (File 5e-10) Complete work sheet

Presented below are selected accounts for Garland Company as reported in the worksheet at the end of May 2002:

	Adjusted trial balance		Income statement		Balance sheet	
	Debit	Credit	Debit	Credit	Debit	Credit
Cash	$9,000					
Merchandise inventory	80,000					
Sales		$450,000				
Sales returns and allowances	10,000					
Sales discounts	7,000					
Cost of goods sold	250,000					

Instructions:
Complete the worksheet by extending amounts reported in the adjusted trial balance to the appropriate columns in the worksheet. Do not total individual columns.

PROBLEMS

Problem P5-1A (File 5p-1a) Journalize purchase and sales transactions under a perpetual inventory system

Travel Warehouse distributes suitcases to retail stores and extends credit terms of 1/10, net/30 to all of its customers. At the end of July, Travel's inventory consisted of 40 suitcases purchased at $40 each. During the month of July the following merchandise transactions occurred:

Jul 1   Purchased 50 suitcases on account for $30 each from Suitcase Manufacturers, FOB destination, terms 1/15, net/30. The appropriate party also made a cash payment of $100 for freight on this date.

Jul 3   Sold 40 suitcases on account to Luggage World for $50 each.

Jul 9   Paid Suitcase Manufacturers in full.

Jul 12   Received payment in full from Luggage World.

Jul 17 Sold 30 suitcases on account to The Travel Spot for $50 each.

Jul 18   Purchased 60 suitcases on account for $1,700 from Vacation Manufacturers, FOB shipping point, terms 2/10, net 30. The appropriate party also made a cash payment of $100 for freight on this date.

Jul 20   Received $300 credit (including freight) for 10 suitcases returned to Vacation Manufacturers.

Jul 21   Received payment in full from The Travel Spot.

Jul 22   Sold 40 suitcases on account to Vacations-Are-Us for $50 each.

Jul 30   Paid Vacation Manufacturers in full.

Jul 31   Granted Vacations-Are-Us $250 credit for 5 suitcases returned costing $150.

Travel Warehouse's chart of accounts includes the following:

Acct Nbr:	Account title:	Acct Nbr:	Account title:
101	Cash	401	Sales
112	Accounts receivable	412	Sales returns and allowances
120	Merchandise inventory	414	Sales discounts
201	Accounts payable	505	Cost of goods sold

Instructions:
Journalize the transactions for the month of July for Travel Warehouse using a perpetual inventory system.

Problem P5-3A (File 5p-3a) Prepare financial statements and adjusting and closing entries

Gitler Department Store is located near the Village shopping mall. At the end of the company's fiscal year on December 31, 2002, the following accounts appeared in two of its trial balances:

Account title	Unadjusted	Adjusted	Account title	Unadjusted	Adjusted
Accounts payable	$79,300	$79,300	Interest revenue	$4,000	$4,000
Accounts receivable	50,300	50,300	Merchandise inventory	75,000	75,000
Accumulated depr-Bldg	42,100	52,500	Mortgage payable	80,000	80,000
Accumulated depr-Equip	29,600	42,900	Office salaries expense	32,000	32,000
Building	190,000	190,000	Prepaid insurance	9,600	2,400
Cash	23,000	23,000	Property taxes expense		4,800
Common stock	110,000	110,000	Property taxes payable		4,800
Cost of goods sold	412,700	412,700	Retained earnings	66,600	66,600
Depreciation exp-Bldg		10,400	Sales salaries expense	76,000	76,000
Depreciation exp-Equip		13,300	Sales	628,000	628,000
Dividends	28,000	28,000	Sales commissions exp	11,000	15,500
Equipment	110,000	110,000	Sales commissions payable		4,500
Insurance expense		7,200	Sales returns & allowances	8,000	8,000
Interest expense	3,000	11,000	Utilities expense	11,000	11,000
Interest payable		8,000			

Analysis reveals the following additional data:
(1) Insurance expense and utilities expense are 60% selling and 40% administrative.
(2) $20,000 of the mortgage payable is due for payment the next year.
(3) Depreciation on building and property tax expense are administrative expenses; depreciation on the equipment is a selling expense.

Instructions:
(a) Prepare a multi-step income statement, a retained earnings statement, and a classified balance sheet.
(b) Journalize the adjusting entries that were made.
(c) Journalize the closing entries that are necessary.

Problem P5-2B (File 5p-2b) Journalize, post, and prepare partial income statement

Eagle Hardware Store Inc. completed the following merchandising transactions in the month of May. At the beginning of May, the ledger of Eagle showed Cash of $5,000 and Common stock of $5,000.

May 1   Purchased merchandise on account from Lathrop Wholesale Supply $6,000, terms 2/10, net 30.

May 2   Sold merchandise on account, $4,700, terms 2/10, net 30. The cost of the merchandise sold was $3,100.

May 5   Received credit from Lathrop Wholesale Supply for merchandise returned $200.

May 9   Received collections in full, less discounts, from customers billed on sales of $4,500 on May.

May 10 Paid Lathrop Wholesale Supply in full, less discount.

May 11 Purchased supplies for cash $900.

May 12 Purchased merchandise for cash $2,400.

May 15 Received refund for poor quality merchandise from supplier on cash purchase $230.

May 17 Purchased merchandise from Kumar Distributors $1,900, FOB shipping point, terms 2/10, net 30.

May 19 Paid freight on May 17 purchase $250.

May 24 Sold merchandise for cash $6,200. The merchandise sold had a cost of $4,340.

May 25 Purchased merchandise from Tsai Inc. $1,000, FOB destination, terms 2/20, net 30.

May 27 Paid Kumar Distributors in full, less discount.

May 29 Made refunds to cash customers for defective merchandise $100. The refunded merchandise had a scrap value of $20.

May 31 Sold merchandise on account $1,600, terms net 30. The cost of the merchandise sold was $1,120.

Eagle Hardware's chart of accounts includes the following:

Acct Nbr:	Account title:	Acct Nbr:	Account title:
101	Cash	311	Common stock
112	Accounts receivable	401	Sales
120	Merchandise inventory	412	Sales returns and allowances
126	Supplies	414	Sales discounts
201	Accounts payable	505	Cost of goods sold

Instructions:

(a) Journalize the transactions utilizing a perpetual inventory system.

(b) Enter the beginning cash and capital balances and post the transactions. (Use J1 for the journal reference.)

(c) Prepare an income statement through gross profit for the month of May 2002.

Problem P5-3B (File 5p-3b) Prepare financial statements and adjusting and closing entries

Forcina Department Store is located in midtown Metropolis. During the past several years, net income has been declining because of suburban shopping centers. At the end of the company's fiscal year on November 30, 2002, the following accounts appeared in two of its trial balances:

Account title	Unadjust	Adjusted	Account title	Unadjust	Adjusted
Accounts payable	$47,310	$47,310	Merchandise inventory	$36,200	$36,200
Accounts receivable	11,770	11,770	Notes payable	46,000	46,000
Accumulated depr-Del equip	15,680	19,680	Prepaid insurance	13,500	4,500
Accumulated depr-Store equip	32,300	41,800	Property taxes expense		3,500
Cash	8,000	8,000	Property taxes payable		3,500
Common stock	70,000	70,000	Rent expense	19,000	19,000
Cost of goods sold	633,220	633,220	Retained earnings	14,200	14,200
Delivery expense	8,200	8,200	Salaries expense	120,000	120,000
Delivery equipment	57,000	57,000	Sales	850,000	850,000
Depreciation exp-Del equip		4,000	Sales commissions exp	8,000	12,750
Depreciation exp-Store equip		9,500	Sales comms payable		4,750
Dividends	12,000	12,000	Sales returns & allow	10,000	10,000
Insurance expense		9,000	Store equipment	125,000	125,000
Interest expense	8,000	8,000	Utilities expense	10,600	10,600
Interest revenue	5,000	5,000			

Analysis reveals the following additional data:
1. Salaries expense is 70% selling and 30% administrative.
2. Insurance expense is 50% selling and 50% administrative.
3. Rent expense, utilities expense, and property tax expense are administrative expenses.
4. Notes payable are due in the year 2005.

Instructions:
(a) Prepare a multi-step income statement, a retained earnings statement, and a classified balance sheet.
(b) Journalize the adjusting entries that were made.
(c) Journalize the closing entries that are necessary.

CHAPTER 6

INVENTORIES

CLUES, HINTS, AND TIPS

Sumif

Excel has many excellent tools to assist in inventory valuation. If the inventory count sheets are entered into Excel worksheets the "Sumif" function can be utilized to find the individual items and sum the total number that appears within the worksheet. The command string for this function is =SUMIF(Reference range, selection criteria, sum range. If the selection criteria is text rather than a number, it must be enclosed within quotation marks. For example, the SumIf function to locate the number 4 within the rage of B2:B100 and then sum the values within the range of C2:C100 would be =SUMIF(B2:B100,4,C2:C100). However, the SumIf function to locate the text string of 011-04-024 within the same range would be =SUMIF(B2:B100,"011-04-024",C2:C100). On the SumIf tab of the chapter 6 file (chptr6) in the data directory is an example of the SumIf function counting apples, berries, and cakes. The caution with this function is that "Apple" and "Apples" are two different text strings so data entry discipline is required.

Filter

Another Excel tool usable in inventory is the "Filter" function. When a worksheet is selected or when specific columns are selected and the path Data>Filter>AutoFilter is followed filters will be imposed on the worksheet by Excel. A filter is a tool to screen and restrict the presentation of data. In the default directory the file chptr6 has a tab "Filter" for demonstration purposes. For this worksheet only Column A was selected for the filter function. Unless restricted, through AutoFilter, Excel will put a filter on every column. While this does not hurt, even if not used or appropriate, only Column A was selected to show that it can be selectively imposed.

When filters are imposed on a worksheet Excel puts an additional button on the top of each column with a filter. This button has an arrow pointing down on it and is contained in the first row of the column. By clicking on this button you activate a drop-down menu showing a complete listing of every text and numerical data entry in the column. In chapter 6 data file, click on "Apples" and all of the items not meeting the criteria of "Apples" in column A are hidden and every row meeting the criteria is moved to the top of the worksheet. This compressed the data and hides the non-relevant data. By clicking on the drop-down arrow again and selecting "All", all of the data is represented in the order that as held before the filter was invoked.

Filters can be placed on every column in the worksheet and multiple criteria filtering is possible. In a worksheet containing parts locations by state, county, city, warehouse, row and rack, you could filter column A to only your part number, then filter column B to the State you wanted, column C to the county, column D to the city, column E to the warehouse. That could easily and quickly take thousands of rows down to one or two. With only one or several columns containing active filters Excel will maintain row integrity of data. That is, Excel moves the entire row when a filtering action is imposed on one column of the worksheet.

Filters are removed in the same manner they are invoked. Follow the path Data>Filter>AutoFilter and they will all be removed. This is called a "Toggled" function – selecting it while it is active turns it off, selecting it while it is off turns it on.

Sort

Excel will also allow multiple layer sorts. In a sort function no data is hidden and the order of presentation has several options. In the chapter 6 data file, chptr6, there is a sort tab to show this function. With sort it is necessary select the worksheet, the columns, the rows, or the cells that you would like sorted. A caution that Excel will usually provide for you is that if selecting less than entire rows, Excel will sort only the selected cells. This may destroy the integrity of the data.

The most convenient way to utilize sort is with titles in row 1 and row 1 frozen through Window>Freeze Pane while row two is highlighted. This will cause Excel to freeze row 1 and help it to be identified as labels. The safest way to utilize the sort function is by selecting all cells within the worksheet by clicking on the select all button above the row 1 number and to the left of the column A letter. After the worksheet is selected follow the path Data>Sort and a pop-up menu will appear. Excel will usually assume that the first row of a frozen pane display is titles so titles will appear as the options. From this menu select Sort by > Item through the drop-down selection pane, Then by > Quantity through the drop-down pane, Then by > Aisle through the drop-down pane. You can select whether you want them in ascending or descending order by clicking on the buttons as you desire. Clicking on OK will result in a sorted worksheet by your selected criteria. Worksheets can be sorted time and time again in different manners without restrictions.

Master Sort Column

The master sort column is a technique rather than an Excel function or formula. If you are going to sort worksheets you may be required to return them to their original order. For example, you have entered 50 inventory sheets into an Excel worksheet for data manipulation. In the process of working with the data you discover what appears to be data entry errors that you want to verify. Once sort has been invoked on a worksheet it is not easy to restore the order. So try putting a Master Sort Column and possible additional sort columns as required. To do this, insert a column at column A by clicking on the column A identifier. Then right click on the highlighted column and select Insert from the options. Excel will insert a new column and push the other columns to the right. The only time it will not do this is every column to the limit of the worksheet has been utilized. Now title that new column Master Sort (or anything else you desire) and insert indexed numbers starting in the first data row. I utilize 2 as my first number to match row numbers to master sort numbers as shown in the chapter 6 data file, chptr6. Drag or fill this column through the data entry range. Now, whenever you need it back into data entry order simply select the worksheet and sort by column A in ascending order.

Suppose that the Director of Sales wants the inventory file in item sort order frequently. Insert a column on top of column B, pushing the existing column B one to the right, and label the column Sales Sort, sort the worksheet. Now, while in sorted presentation, put numbers into column B as you did in column A with the master sort. Now any time the Director of Sales wants his presentation, select the worksheet and sort by column B in ascending order. Remember that as the data within the worksheet changes, the sort may need to be run and the sort index may need to be refreshed. Any party requesting special presentation of the data can have their own sort row and these rows need not be printed by excluding them from the print area.

EXERCISES

Exercise E6-3 (File 6e-3) Prepare an income statement

Presented is information related to Boliva Co. for the month of January 2002:

Freight-in	$10,000	Rent expense	$19,000
Freight-out	5,000	Salaries expense	61,000
Insurance expense	12,000	Sales discounts	8,000
Purchases	220,000	Sales returns & allowances	13,000
Purchases discounts	3,000	Sales	325,000
Purchases returns & allowances	6,000		

Beginning merchandise inventory was $42,000. Ending merchandise inventory was $63,000.

Instructions:
Prepare an income statement using the format provided below. Operating expenses should not be segregated into selling and administrative expenses.

Sales revenues
    Sales
        Less: Sales returns and allowances

Sales discounts
Net sales
Cost of goods sold
    Inventory, January 1
    Purchases
    Less: Purchases returns and allowances
            Purchases discounts
      Net purchases
    Add: Freight-in
      Cost of goods purchased
        Cost of goods available for sale
          Inventory, January 31
Cost of goods sold
   Gross profit
Operating expenses
   Salaries expense
   Rent expense
   Insurance expense
   Freight-out
     Total operating expenses
Net Income

Exercise E6-11 (File 6e-11) Compute inventory turnover, days in inventory, and gross profit rate.

This information is available for Wideangle Lens Corporation for 2000, 2001, and 2002:

	2000	2001	2002
Beginning inventory	$200,000	$300,000	$400,000
Ending inventory	300,000	400,000	500,000
Cost of goods sold	850,000	1,120,000	1,200,000
Sales	1,200,000	1,600,000	1,900,000

Instructions:
Calculate inventory turnover, days in inventory, and gross profit rate (from chapter 5 of the text book) for Wideangle Lens Corporation for 2000, 2001, and 2002. Comment on any trends.

Exercise E6-12 (File 6e-12) Determine merchandise lost using the gross profit method of estimating inventory

The inventory of Odeon Company was destroyed by fire on March 1. From an examination of the accounting records, the following data for the first two months of the year are obtained:

Sales	$51,000
Sales returns & allowances	1,000
Purchases	28,200
Freight-in	1,200
Purchases returns & allowances	1,400

Instructions:

(a) Determine the merchandise lost by fire, assuming a beginning inventory of $25,000 and a gross profit rate of 30% on net sales.

(b) Determine the merchandise lost by fire, assuming a beginning inventory of $30,000 and a gross profit rate of 25% on net sales.

PROBLEMS

Problem P6-1A (File 6p-1a) Journalize, post, and prepare a trial balance and partial income statement

Vanessa Williams, a professional tennis star, operates VW's Tennis Shop at the Florida Lake Resort. At the beginning of the current season, the ledger of VW's Tennis Shop showed cash - $2,500, Merchandise inventory - $1,700, and Common stock - $4,200. The following transactions were completed during April 2002.

Apr 4   Purchased racquets and balls from Daddy Co. $840 FOB shipping point, terms 3/10, net 30.

Apr 6   Paid freight on Daddy Co. purchase $40.

Apr 8   Sold merchandise to members $900, terms net 30.

Apr 10 Received credit of $40 from Daddy Co. for a damaged racquet that was returned.

Apr 11 Purchased tennis shoes from Niki Sports for cash $300.

Apr 13 Paid Daddy Co. in full.

Apr 14 Purchased tennis shirts and shorts from Martina's Sportswear $900 FOB shipping point, terms 2/10, net 60.

Apr 15 Received cash refund of $50 from Niki Sports for damaged merchandise that was returned.

Apr 17 Paid freight on Martina's Sportswear purchase $30.

Apr 18 Sold merchandise to members $800, terms net 30.

Apr 20 Received $500 in cash from members in settlement of their accounts.

Apr 21 Paid Martina's Sportswear in full.

Apr 27 Granted credit to $30 to members for tennis clothing that did not fit.

Apr 30 Sold merchandise to members $900, terms net 30.

Apr 30 Received cash payments on account from members $500.

The chart of accounts for the tennis shop includes the following:

Acct Nbr:	Account title:	Acct Nbr:	Account title:
101	Cash	412	Sales returns & allowances
112	Accounts receivable	510	Purchases
120	Merchandise inventory	512	Purchases returns & allowances
201	Accounts payable	514	Purchases discounts
311	Common stock	516	Freight-in
401	Sales		

Instructions:

(a) Journalize the April transactions using a periodic inventory system.

(b) Enter the beginning balances in the ledger accounts and post the April transactions. (Use J1 for the

50   Solving Financial Accounting Problems Using Excel For Windows

journal reference.)
(c) Prepare a trial balance on April 30, 2002.
(d) Prepare an income statement through gross profit, assuming merchandise inventory on hand at
April 30, 2002 is $1,800.

Problem P6-6A (File 6p-6a) Compute ending inventory and cost of inventory lost using retail method

Korean Department Store uses the retail inventory method to estimate its monthly ending inventories. The following information is available for two of its departments at *August 31, 2002*:

| | Sporting Goods | | Jewelry & Cosmetics | |
	Cost	Retail	Cost	Retail
Net sales		$1,010,000		$1,150,000
Purchases	$670,000	1,066,000	$733,000	1,158,000
Purchases returns & allowances	(26,000)	(40,000)	(12,000)	(20,000)
Purchases discounts	(15,360)		(9,440)	
Freight-in	6,000		8,000	
Beginning inventory	47,360	74,000	36,440	62,000

At *December 31*, Korean Department Store takes a physical inventory at retail. The actual retail values of the inventories in each department are Sporting Goods - $85,000, and Jewelry & Cosmetics – $54,000.

Instructions:
(a) Determine the estimated cost of the ending inventory for each department on *August 31, 2002* using the retail inventory method.
(b) Compute the ending inventory at cost for each department at *December 31, 2002*, assuming the cost-to-retail ratios are 60% for sporting goods and 65% for jewelry & cosmetics.

Problem P6-2B (File 6p-2b) Prepare an income statement

Bedazzle Department Store is located in midtown Metropolis. During the past several years, net income has been declining because of suburban shopping centers. At the end of the company's fiscal year on November 30, 2002, the following accounts appeared in its adjusted trial balance:

Account title	Balance	Account title	Balance
Accounts payable	$35,310	Prepaid insurance	$4,500
Accounts receivable	11,770	Property taxes expense	3,500
Accumulated depr-Delivery equip	19,680	Purchases	650,000
Accumulated depr-Store equip	41,800	Purchases discounts	7,000
Cash	8,000	Purchase returns & allowances	3,000
Delivery expense	8,200	Rent expense	19,000
Delivery equipment	57,000	Salaries expense	150,000
Depreciation exp-Delivery equip	4,000	Sales	910,000
Depreciation expense-Store equip	9,500	Sales commissions exp	12,000
Freight-in	5,060	Sales commissions payable	8,000
Common stock	70,000	Sales returns & allowances	10,000
Retained earnings	17,200	Store equipment	125,000

Dividends	12,000	Property taxes payable	3,500
Insurance expense	34,360	Utilities expense	10,600
Notes payable	46,000		

Analysis reveals the following additional data:
    (1) Salaries expense is 70% selling and 30% administrative.
    (2) Insurance expense is 50% selling and 50% administrative.
    (3) Merchandise inventory at November 30, 2002, is $36,200.
    (4) Rent expense, utilities expense, and property tax expense are administrative expenses.

Instructions:
Prepare an income statement for the year ended November 30, 2002.

Problem P6-6B (File 6p-6b) Compute ending inventory using retail method

Enlighten Book Store uses the retail inventory method to estimate its monthly ending inventories. The following information is available for two of its departments at *October 31, 2002*:

	Hardcovers		Paperbooks	
	Cost	Retail	Cost	Retail
Beginning inventory	$260,000	$400,000	$65,000	$90,000
Purchases	1,180,000	1,800,000	266,000	380,000
Freight-in	5,000		2,000	
Purchases discounts	15,000		4,000	
Net sales		1,820,000		368,000

At *December 31*, Enlighten takes a physical inventory at retail. The actual retail values of the inventories in each department are Hardcovers - $400,000, and Paperbacks – $95,000.

Instructions:
(a) Determine the estimated cost of the ending inventory for each department on *October 31, 2002*, using the retail inventory method.
(b) Compute the ending inventory at cost for each department at *December 31, 2002*, assuming the cost-to-retail ratios are 65% for hardcovers and 70% for paperbacks.

CHAPTER 7

ACCOUNTING PRINCIPLES

CLUES, HINTS, AND TIPS

Name ranges

Excel will allow you to name a range as shown on the Chapter 7 data file, chptr7, in the data directory. Open the file and click into the Intermediate Formulas tab for this example. For Excel a named range is a single cell or multiple cells identified through the naming process with a unique name. This name has some controls and restrictions such as no spaces and only a couple of special characters. To name a cell or range of adjacent cells, highlight the individual cell or for a range click into the upper left, upper right, lower left, or lower right cell and sweep the range. If the range is not adjacent cells, click into the first cell and highlight it or highlight the first range, then release the mouse button, press and hold the control key down and click into the second cell or highlight the second range, release the mouse button, continue to hold the control key down and continue to highlight the cells or ranges with the mouse releasing only the mouse button after each cell or section. Then follow the path Insert>Name>Define and enter your chosen name in the pop-up dialog box. You can see the defined cells in the "Refers to" window at the bottom of the box. You can also enter the name directly into Excel by clicking into the cell identity box on the formula bar and entering it. By clicking into this box you will also see the other named ranges for the worksheet.

In the chapter 7 data worksheet the ranges have been named for their fill colors. The ranges of Red, Yellow, Blue, and Green are all adjacent cells for their ranges. The range Purple is non-adjacent cells and had values inserted in the nonparticipating cells. Excel will not include these values in the summation and math functions utilized by formulas calling for the range Purple. The cell A25 contains a formula summing all of the cells within the range of A18 through A24. This value is 63. However, only the cells A18, A20, A22, and A24 are considered and identified as participants within the range name Purple. The sum of Purple is only 36 as shown in cell C19 and cell B25.

To the right of the cells are formulas showing different ways of summing the values of the cells. As you can see, you can address the range of Red several ways – A1+A2+A3+A4, A1:A4, or Red. You can see how Excel will add the values of Red and Yellow together and how it will add the rest of the ranges together as well as you look down columns C and D of the worksheet.

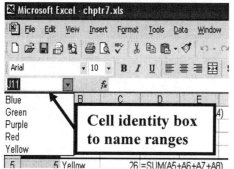

As addressed earlier in the booklet, the prefix of =SUM(starts Excel into the "I have to do something with formulas and functions" mode. When a formula is embedded within another formula, the equal sign "=" is not used and will cause an error message to appear. The chapter 7 data file Embedded Formula tab has examples of these formulas. A simple embedded formula is stated as: if the value in column B for the row is Red, than add the value of column A. This formula is written as: =IF(B1="Red",sum(A1)). Note the single parenthesis to start the formula, the single parenthesis to start the identify the cell A1 and the double parenthesis to end the formula – the first or left most, to contain the identity of the cell A1 and the second, the outer parenthesis to contain the formula, the matching or closing parenthesis from the start of the formula. This formula is in cell D1 of the chapter 7 data file, chptr7. Formulas and functions can be embedded to 7 layers within Excel. That is, if you have more than 7 opening and closing parenthesis, you may get an error message from Excel. (Remember that your opening and closing parenthesis must remain matched.) This is not much of a restriction since you can write another logic formula or math formula based on the results of the first formula or function.

Virtually every formula or function of Excel can be embedded within another. In the templates functions such as concatenate are used to write journal entry narratives based on the existence of an entry in the date column. The summing of the ledger accounts are embedded formulas based on the date column being empty or null, or as Excel states it "". When writing embedded formulas it is usually best to start out with the end result formula or function and ensure it provides the expected response to the data, then build the evaluators and logic statements in front of it.

Intermediate formulas

Excel has many built in formulas and functions which can be found through the F_x icon on the tool or task bar. Shown below is the dialog box that is presented when you click on the F_x icon. This dialog box provides an index of most of the structured Excel formulas and functions. A very nice feature of this dialog box is that it gives you a brief summary of actions and capabilities of the formula or function in the lower third of the dialog box. This is a handy feature when scrolling through the formulas trying to find a fit for your need. In the screen print below the function or formula for SumIf is selected. The dialog box tells you that it adds the cells specified by a given condition or criteria. Exactly what we were seeking in the chapter 6 tasking for the valuation of inventory.

This dialog box can be narrowed down in its search through the selection made in the "or select a category" window in the upper third of the dialog box. The categories include financial, math & trig, statistics, lookup and reference, text, and logical. Selecting one of these categories will narrow your search but may preclude you from seeing a viable option contained under another category.

Formulas and functions in Excel normally start with the equal sign, "=", which keys Excel into expecting to accomplish something. From this point text, data, and reference information is provided. The simple Excel formula of =I2, a "Look to" formula or function, placed in cell J1 would simply provide you with the contents of cell I1 being presented again in cell J1 as shown on the Chapter 7 Intermediate Formulas tab in the data file chptr7. Excel will also do "Look to" on text values as shown in cells I2 and J2.

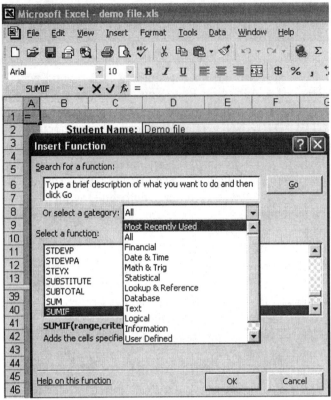

When text is incorporated as part of a formula or function within Excel it must be enclosed within quotation marks or Excel will product an error message. In the logic formula shown in cell D1 on the Embedded Formulas tab of the chapter 7 data file, you will see the word Red within quotation marks. In the cell D2 the same formula has been written to read the contents of cell B2 and compare it to the value of Red. If the comparison is a match, the formula should return the value contained within cell A2. Excel has made the determination that Red in the formula is a math statement while Red in cell B2 is a text entry, since text and math statements are not equal, Excel simply states "False", Red as a math function does not equal Red as a text statement. This is an expected and acceptable return. If you wanted the sum of cell A2 if B2 was the text entry of Red, you should have put Red in the formula within quotation marks.

Occasionally Excel will have problems with formulas that should yield specific results. The often effective solution is to insure that the formatting of the cells is not precluding the formula or function action. For example, click into cell G4 of the chapter 7 data file Embedded Formula tab. Once the cell is active, click on the Omega symbol (Σ) for quick sum and Excel looks over to column A and generates a formula of =SUM(A4:F4) while you would have expected Excel to generate a formula of =SUM(G1:G3). After all, cells G1 through G3 have the numbers 1, 2, and 3 in them respectively. However, the key to Excel's response is that the cell range G1 through I11 has been formatted to Text. Excel no longer recognized the numbers within this range as math statements. They are now text statements.

Excel has a solution for the problem of text entry. On the Chapter 7 data file Embedded Formula tab, column J, rows 1 through 3 is the Excel function of "Value". This function converts numerical presentation of text into math statements. As shown below, in cell J4, there is a formula that adds these values up correctly while they can not be added within the text defined range of G1 through I11. The value function is found in the Text category of functions.

Scrolling through the All formulas and functions category of Excel will reveal many useful formulas and functions applicable to the exercises and problems of the text book. However, Excel is a tool and the results of every Excel formula and function needs to be evaluated for reasonableness. When working on extensive and intricate data proof the concept with basic data and simple values. For example, with the DDB function to handle double-declining depreciation of an asset, verify it with a $10,000 asset, $0.00 salvage value, 5 year life at 200%. This should return a value of 40% of $10,000 (100% / 5 year life X 200%) or $4,000 for the first period. If another value is returned, something is wrong with the formula selection, the data input or formatting. In this formula, Excel is not expecting 200 for 200%, it is expecting either "2" for twice straight-line or "200%". Excel also is not expecting commas to be entered into the values.

Tip – while working on formulas and functions, you can insert a single text character in front of the equal sign and the formula or function becomes a text string and will not process. This is a handy "escape" while troubleshooting problems and situations that may arise during entry. Excel does not want you to leave the cell with a formula or function it can not handle. It will present you with proposed resolutions and trouble screens. By inserting a character in front of the equal sign this can be stopped. As a matter of presentation, if the character is a single or double quote, Excel will not show that character in the display of the cell data. This makes the single or double quote presentation neat and clean. You can see many of these inserts through the data files.

Concatenate

Concatenate is a text function of Excel. Concatenate is the function for joining two or more text strings into a single cell. On the chapter 7 data file Concatenate tab you will find a string of text entered into the individual cells of column A. In cell B1 the concatenate function is written as:

=CONCATENATE(A1," ",A2," ",A3," ",A4," ",A5," ",SUM(A6+A8)," ",A10,"s.")

This function shows that it is taking the contents of cell A1, placing a space as shown by the " " presentation, then showing the contents of cell A2 and so on. However, the text string shows that the fox jumped over the sum of 4 and 7 dogs. Concatenate will accept the formula to sum these, but remember that this is embedding a formula inside a formula or function so an equal sign is not appropriate and its presence will create an error code. The function finishes with the final text being brought into the string. The last text entry within concatenate handles the issue that the word "dog" in cell A10 is singular while the quantity of more than one dog is plural. This line adds an "s" to dog and adds the period to finish the sentence. Features such as this insert text, formula, and functions really make concatenate a powerful function.

To enter spaces within concatenate simply strike the space bar once or more (if more than one space is desired) and then tab to the next data entry area. Each cell must be referenced on its own line for text to be inserted. When Concatenate opens it may only give you one or two data entry fields, as you fill one and strike tab to move to the next, additional fields will appear. Concatenate generated strings are dependent on the reference cells. So, by changing the word "dog" to "house" in cell A10 you will change the concatenate string as you invoke the change by exiting the cell. For a solution to this, see the next Clue, Hint, and Tip – Paste special.

Paste special

When you generate a formula within Excel it is dynamic, dependent upon its reference cells. As shown in the concatenate function, changing a cell will change the text string produced by the function. There is a way to stop this without retyping or reentering all of the data. Copy the target cell, in this case, click into cell B4 on the Concatenate tab of the chapter 7 data file. This cell contains a live formula or function of Excel. In the formula window you will see the presentation of the formula. Use the key strokes Ctrl-C, click on the copy icon (two overlaying sheets) on the task bar, follow the path Edit>Copy, or right click and select the "Copy" option from the pop-up menu to copy the cell. This copies the formula or function onto the Windows clipboard. Place your cursor back over the B4 cell and right click the cell to get a pop-up menu or follow the path Edit>Paste Special to get the same pop-up menu. From the pop-up menu, shown here, select the Paste Values option and click OK. At this point Excel will replace the formula or function with the results of the formula or function. The concatenate function is gone, the resulting string

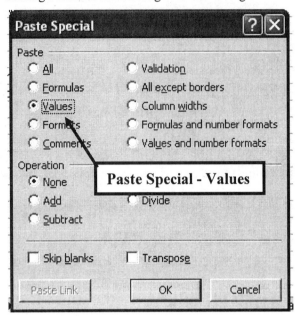

is no longer dependent upon the parent cells. So changing cell A10, the word "dog" to "house" will not change this string any farther.

This is a handy function for worksheets that are going to be distributed to individuals who like to "play" with your extensive formulas and functions. By selecting the entire sheet, copying, and pasting the data back through Paste Special the data will be static and not dependent upon the source cells. This feature or function also helps when the values within the worksheet are built on values contained within other worksheets that the recipient does not have access to.

EXERCISES

Exercise E7-5 (File 7e-5) Compute earnings per share

The ledger of Batavia Corporation at December 31, 2002, contains the following summary information:

Administrative expenses	$112,000	Other expenses & losses	$34,700
Cost of goods sold	409,200	Other revenues & gains	17,500
Net sales	682,000	Selling expenses	98,600

The income tax rate for all items is 30%. Batavia had 10,000 shares of common stock outstanding throughout the year, and the company paid $15,000 in dividends during 2002.

Instructions:
Compute earnings per share for 2002.

Exercise E7-6 (File 7e-6) Prepare an income statement and calculate related information

Presented below, in alphabetical order, is information related to Aurora Corporation for the year 2002:

Cost of goods sold	$1,499,900	Interest expense	$90,000
Dividends on common stock	140,000	Interest revenue	300,000
Gain on sale of equipment	110,000	Net sales	2,142,800
Income tax expense	150,000	Selling and administrative expenses	340,750

Aurora had 35,000 shares outstanding for the entire year.

Instructions:
(a) Prepare in good form a single-step income statement for Aurora Corporation for 2002.
(b) Assuming a multiple-step income statement was prepared instead of, compute:
    (1) Gross profit.
    (2) Income from operations.
    (3) Net income.
(c) Calculate Aurora Corporation's profit margin percentage (return on sales).

PROBLEMS

Problem P7-4A (File 7p-4a) Prepare a classified balance sheet and analyze financial position

The adjusted trial balance of Madonna Plastic Boat, Inc., as of June 30, 2002 (its fiscal year end) contains the following information:

Accounts payable	$478,000
Accounts receivable	420,000
Accumulated depreciation-Building	180,000
Accumulated depreciation-Equipment	577,500
Bonds payable	1,750,000
Building-Mfg plant & offices	680,000
Cash	79,000
Common stock	500,000
Equipment	1,650,000
Income taxes payable	45,000
Interest payable	70,000
Interest receivable	21,000
Inventories	845,000
Investment in Spartan, Inc., bonds (Held-to-maturity, Long term)	600,000
Land	200,000
Mortgage payable	310,000
Notes payable - short-term	200,000
Prepaid advertising	9,500
Prepaid insurance	21,000
Retained earnings, June 30, 2002	447,000
Supplies	32,000

Instructions:
(a) Prepare in good form a classified balance sheet for Madonna Plastic Boat, Inc.
(b) Calculate the following balance sheet relationships:
    (1) Current ratio.
    (2) Debt-to-total assets ratio.
    (3) Working capital.
(c) Assume that Madonna has come to you, as vice president of Illinois National Bank, seeking a $450,000 loan to help defray the costs of upgrading some of its machinery. Would you be willing to

approve the loan? Is there any additional information you would like to have before making your decision?

Problem P7-5A (File 7p-5a) Prepare a multiple-step income statement and analyze profitability

The ledgers of Larry's Leathers Inc. contain the following balances as of January 31, 2002 (the end of its fiscal year).

Advertising expense	$129,000
Depreciation exp-administrative	53,000
Freight-in	27,900
Freight-out	6,800
Gain on sale of equipment	8,500
Insurance expense	54,000
Interest expense	13,900
Interest revenue	7,300
Inventory, February 1, 2001	296,400
Inventory, January 31, 2002	303,400
Managerial salaries	129,800
Miscellaneous admin expenses	22,200
Miscellaneous selling expenses	39,000
Net purchases	1,697,000
Net sales	2,647,000
Rent expense	81,000
Sales staff wages	159,000
Utilities expense	30,300

Income taxes are calculated at 30 percent of income. Larry's had 84,000 shares of common stock outstanding for the entire year. Total assets amounted to $5,460,000, and common stockholders' equity was $1,966,200 at year end.

Instructions:
(a) Prepare in good form a multiple-step income statement for Larry's Leathers Inc.
(b) Calculate three measures of profitability and one ratio of solvency.
(c) Assume that you are considering supplying Larry's Leathers with a line wallets, key holders, and other small leather goods for sale in its two stores. Is this a company for which you would like to be a supplier? What additional information would you like to have before deciding to become a supplier for Larry's Leathers?

CHAPTER 8

INTERNAL CONTROL AND CASH

CHAPTER OUTLINE

CLUES, HINTS, AND TIPS

Absolute reference

Excel has a feature called "Absolute reference". This function will maintain cell reference by column, row, or both when the formula or function is moved. To understand the function, you need to appreciate how Excel copies and moves things. On the chapter 8 data file Absolute Reference tab there is a small range of number and some formulas to show how Excel handles copy and paste as well as move. In cell C1 the formula is totally relational. While the formula reads =A1+A2+A3, what Excel really is saying is look two columns to the left (formula in column C, first value in column A,) then, do not change rows, (both formula and first row reference is row 1), and add that value to the value two columns to the left and one row below the formula row, and add that sum to the value found in the cell two columns to the left, and two rows down. To prove this concept out, click into cell C1 to make it the active cell and then use the key strokes Ctrl-C, right click the cell and select the copy option off the pop-up menu, or follow the path Edit>Copy to copy the formula (contents) of the cell. Now move your cursor over to cell F1 and click into cell F1, activating that cell. Now right click the cell and select paste from the pop-up menu, follow the path Edit>Paste, or utilize the key strokes Ctrl-V to paste the formula into cell F1. When you complete the paste operation, the value returned by the formula is #VALUE because you are telling Excel to add three text strings contained in cells C1 through C3 together and that is obviously an error of procedure. That is because you moved the formula 3 columns to the right and now Excel is looking at cells C1 through C3 – the same relationship that cells A1 through A3 held to cell C1. They are 2 columns to the left and one the formula row, one under the formula row, and two under the formula row.

Click back into the cell C1 and copy the formula again. This time paste the formula into cell F5. This time the formula returns the value of 0 or zero since it is now looking at cells C5 through C7 and there is nothing contained within those cells. The relationship of cells C5 through C7 are the same to F5 as the relationship of cells A1 through A3 are to cell C1 and cells C1 through C3 are to F1 – two columns to the left and on the formula row, one down, and two rows down. This is relational movement.

To overcome relational movement factors Excel allows you to place a special character – the dollar sign ($) in front of the column identifier, the row identifier, or both the column and row identifier. On the Absolute reference tab of the chapter 7 data file click into cell C2, this formula is absolute reference to the column only and is relational to the row. The formula is =$A1+$A2+$A3. Copy the formula and paste it into cell F2 and watch the results. This time the formula returns a valid answer of 6. Examine the formula in cell F2 and you will see that the column reference has remained at A and the rows have remained at 1 through 3 since your original formula was on row 2 and the pasted formula is on row 2. Click back into cell C2 and copy the formula. This time paste the formula into cell F6. This time the formula become =$A5+$A6+$A7. It maintained is column reference because of the dollar signs but the rows shifted. In cell C2 the formula looks one row up, then on its row, then one row down. Now on row 6 it is looking one row up, to row 5, looking at its row, row 6, and one row down to row 7 and summing the values – no value so no product within those cells. The formula maintained absolute column and relational row references.

In cell C3 the formula is written with relational column references and absolute row references. This is done by writing the formula as =A$1+A$2+A$3. Experiment with copying and pasting this formula around the worksheet. The row references will always be 1, 2, and 3 but the column references will change by your relationship between column C and where you paste it. Try pasting it into column A or B and watch the results. Since the reference was to two to the left of column C, when pasted into column A or B the relational column is to the left of column A, a place in cyber space the formula does not have access to.

By writing the formula as =$A$1+$A$2+$A$3 both the column and row are absolute reference and not relational. Copy this formula as shown in cell C4 to other locations on the worksheet and watch the results and resulting formula. Try pasting the formula into column A or B and watch the results. Since the references are absolute and not relational, the results are valid.

You can mix absolute and relational references as shown. Plus, you can absolute reference one value and relational the next. For example, there is a mini tax table on the Absolute Reference tab. The formula was placed into cell C10 was written to absolute reference the tax rate cell, cell C8, and then relational reference the purchase amount in column A starting at row 10. The formula was then dragged down the column. In the drag process, it maintained the absolute and relational references and produced the tax amount.

Copying a formula

Excel has several ways of copying formulas and functions. Most of them are considered "relational" in their operation. These are explained in detail in the preceding Absolute Reference section. The quickest and easiest way to copy a formula within Excel is to click into the cell containing the formula and use any of the numerous ways to copy within Excel. Then move into the target cell and paste the formula there via any of the numerous ways to paste within Excel. However, these are relational copying processes. To copy the formula and not have it read relational to its target cell requires a little bit of technique unless the formula is absolute referenced. Click into the cell with the formula. In the formula window at the top of the screen, click into the formula window and then sweep from right to left with the left mouse button down the entire formula window. When the entire formula in the formula window is highlighted, use any of the copy commands of Excel to copy the data. Move to the target cell and click into it to make it the active cell. Now paste the formula into the cell with any of the paste commands of Excel. The formula is now in the target cell with its original references, not relationally moved.

This technique will also allow you to copy a formula out of one cell and paste it into another cell as part of that formula. If you are building embedded formulas, as addressed earlier, you can proof the formula segment in one cell, use this concept to copy that segment and then paste it into the embedded formula cell.

Cut Command

The "cut" command is accessible from the key strokes Ctrl-X, the path Edit>Cut, right click on the cell or range of cells once they are highlighted and select it from the pop-up menu, or click on the scissors icon on the tool bar. To cut a cell or a range of cells, highlight the cell or range of cells. If the cells are not adjacent to each other you will have to do more than one cut operation to get them as cut will not accept nonadjacent cells. When you cut a cell or range of cells from an Excel worksheet they will not disappear immediately from the worksheet. They will remain encircled by a dancing daisy chain until you paste them into their new location. When you use the paste command to put the cells in the new location you will not receive any warning about over printing existing data. If you want to place the data in more than one location you will have to highlight it again, easy since it will be highlighted immediately after the paste operation, then copy it and place it in the new location. Cut is a one time operation, you can paste several copies of a cell or range of cells from a copy operation but not from a cut operation.

When you cut a cell containing a formula with the cut command and paste it into a new location the formula retains its original references even if it is not relational.

A feature associated with cut is the insert function. The function is found under the path Insert>Cut Cells or by right clicking on a cell after the cut command has been utilized. If a column, row, range, or individual cell has been cut, this feature will insert it in relation to its shape and the target cell as instructed. If the positioning is not clear to Excel a dialog box may appear that asks if you want the cut cells inserted, pushing the existing cells to the right or down. Formulas associated with the cut cells will be updated to the new location of their reference data. Cut will not remove a cell, range, column, or row from the worksheet. The delete function will accomplish that. Also, if the cut command is initiated and not completed with a paste command, the data will not be removed from the worksheet.

Delete and Delete

There are actually two deletes within Excel. The first is the keyboard delete key. This key will simply remove data from the worksheet. Any formula referencing the deleted cells may or may not continue to work correctly. This depends on how the formula works and where the value of the deleted cell was in the formula. If the formula added the values contained within three cells together and then divided that sum by the value in a fourth cell and one of the numerator values is deleted the formula should continue to work. If the denominator was deleted the formula will error out since division by zero and null values is undefined.

The second delete is from the path Edit>Delete or the pop-up menu found by right clicking a cell, range of cells, a row or range of rows, or a column or range of columns. When this option is used the selected cell or cells disappear. This command will frequently result in a pop-up dialog box asking what movement you would like to occur as the cells are deleted – would you like them moved up or to the left.

These are two totally different functions – the delete key clears data but does not clear formatting, the delete selection on the pop-up menu or the path Edit>Delete makes cells disappear and causes the worksheet to be repositioned. All of these actions are reversible until the save function in invoked. The save function resets the Undo capability.

EXERCISES

Exercise E8-5 (File 8e-5) Prepare journal entries for a petty cash fund

Leland Company uses an imprest petty cash system. The fund was established on March 1 with a balance of $100. During March the following petty cash receipts were found in the petty cash box:

Date	Receipt Nbr	For	Amount
3/5	1	Stamp inventory	$35
3/7	2	Freight-out	19
3/9	3	Miscellaneous expenses	12
3/11	4	Travel expense	24
3/14	5	Miscellaneous expenses	5

The fund was replenished on March 15th when the fund contained $4 in cash. On March 20th, the amount of the fund was increased to $150.

Instructions:
Journalize the entries in March that pertain to the operation of the petty cash fund.

Exercise E8-8 (File 8e-8) Prepare a bank reconciliation and adjusting entries

The following information pertains to Cody Video Company:
1. Cash balance per bank, July 31, $7,263.
2. July bank service charge not recorded by the depositor $15.
3. Cash balance per books, July 31, $7,190.
4. Deposits in transit, July 31, $1,500.
5. Bank collected $800 note for Cody in July, plus interest $36, less fee $20. The collection has not been recorded by Cody, and no interest has been accrued.
6. Outstanding checks, July 31, $772.

Instructions:
(a) Prepare a bank reconciliation at July 31.
(b) Journalize the adjusting entries at July 31 on the books of Cody Video Company.

PROBLEMS

Problem P8-3A (File 8p-3a) Prepare bank reconciliation and adjusting entries

On May 31, 2002, Sosa Company had a cash balance per books of $6,781.50. The bank statement from Sandwich Community Bank on that date showed a balance of $6,804.60. A comparison of the statement with the cash account revealed the following facts:
1. The statement includes a debit memo of $40 for the printing of additional company checks.
2. Cash sales of $836.15 on May 12 were deposited in the bank. The cash receipts journal entry and the deposit slip were incorrectly made for $846.15. The bank credited Sosa Company for the correct amount.
3. Outstanding checks at May 31 totaled $276.25. Deposits in transit were $1,936.15.
4. On May 18, the company issued check no. 1181 for $685 to Kap Shin, on account. The check, which cleared the bank in May, was incorrectly journalized and posted to Sosa Company for $685.
5. A $3,000 note receivable was collected by the bank for Sosa Company on May 31 plus $80 interest. The bank charged a collection fee of $20. No interest has been accrued on the note.
6. Included with the cancelled checks was a check issued by Tacamoto Company to Yee Chow for $600 that was incorrectly charged to Sosa Company by the bank.
7. On May 31, the bank statement shows an NSF charge of $700 for a check issued by John Lewis, a customer, to Sosa Company on account.

Instructions:
(a) Prepare the bank reconciliation at May 31, 2002.
(b) Prepare the necessary adjusting entries for Sosa Company at May 31, 2002.

Problem P8-5A (File 8p-5a) Prepare bank reconciliation and adjusting entries

Videosoft Company maintains a checking account at the Intelex Bank. At July 31, selected data from the ledger balance and the bank statement are as follows:

	Cash in bank	
	Per books	Per bank
Balance, July 1	$17,600	$18,800
July receipts	82,000	
July credits		80,470
July disbursements	76,900	
July debits		74,740
Balance, July 31	$22,700	$24,530

Analysis of the bank data reveals that the credits consist of $79,000 of July deposits and a credit memorandum of $1,470 for the collection of a $1,400 note plus interest revenue of $70. The July debits per bank consist of checks cleared $74,700 and a debit memorandum of $40 for printing additional company checks.
You also discover the following errors involving July checks:
(1) A check for $230 to a creditor on account that cleared the bank in July was journalized and posted as $320.

(2) A salary check to an employee for $255 was recorded by the bank for $155.

The June 30 bank reconciliation contained only two reconciling items:

(1) Deposits in transit of $5,000.

(2) Outstanding checks of $6,200.

Instructions:

(a) Prepare a bank reconciliation at July 31.

(b) Journalize the adjusting entries to be made by Videosoft Company at July 31, 2002. Assume that the interest on the note has been accrued.

CHAPTER 9

ACCOUNTING FOR RECEIVABLES

CLUES, HINTS, AND TIPS

Comments

Frequently the presentation of purely numerical data is insufficient for the effective communication of financial data within a worksheet. At other times you want to document where the data came from or what the data represents. Excel, as shown, will accept text entry into the cells easily and effectively as you have vast formatting capabilities of that text and numerical data. But Excel presents you with another very effective text presentation mode referred to as Comments. Comments are "Pop-up" blocks associated with a particular cell. They can contain a wide variety of information and the text within the block can be formatted with many of the commands and features found elsewhere in Excel. The chapter 9 data file, chptr9, contains comments on the Comments tab as examples of what can be done with comments. These examples can be and are extreme for presentation purposes. Comments have tool bar icons on the Review Tool bar or menu listing.

To attach a comment to a cell follow the path Insert>Comment, right click on the target cell and select Insert Comment, or click on the New Comment icon on the tool bar – an envelope with a ray from the upper left corner. The comment box will pop-up attached to the cell. Contained inside the comment box will be the owner's name of the Excel program by default. This name can be left or removed. The name has been removed from a couple of the comments attached to the worksheet. To remove the ownership name from the comment box simply highlight the text and delete it with the delete key. Enter the text and data as you desire. The comment box can be resized to show only part or all of its comments. It can also be repositioned as to the location that it appears in. When the data entry is complete simply click on the worksheet outside the comment box and the comment box will disappear. Any cell with a comment attached will bear a red triangle in the upper right corner. You can place your cursor over a comment triangle and the comment will pop-up and remain in view until you reposition the cursor. If you desire to edit the comment follow the path Insert>Edit Comment, right click on the cell and select the Edit Comment option, or click on the Edit Comment icon on the tool bar – an envelope with a pencil writing on it. In the edit mode you can still resize or reposition the comment box or reformat the contents. There is an icon to display all comments and to hide all comments with one key click. There is also a Delete Comment icon on the tool bar. Delete comment is also available through right clicking the cell and selecting that option.

Linking worksheets

Excel can utilize the "Look to" function as a quick link between worksheets within the same workbook and link between worksheets in difference workbooks. This is different than a true link or hyperlink which provides the path to the target document. If you are working within the same workbook but different worksheets within Excel simply enter the equal sign into the target cell, select the source worksheet and click into the source cell. This is demonstrated in the chapter 9 data file on the Linked to Comments tab. In cell A1 the equal sign was entered, then the Comments worksheet was selected and Enter was struck. This returns you to the Linked to Comments worksheet. Then the formula was dragged down through cell A5. The dragging operation was relational as explained under Absolute References so the cells A1 through A5 of the Linked to Comments tab are now "children" or "dependents" of the "parent" or "source" cells of the Comments tab.

Notice the special format and sequence of the linking formula, =Comments!A1. This can be typed in manually if desired but it is quicker and less troublesome to let Excel write the formula. You can utilize these cells for data within other formulas and you can add functions and formulas to the linking formula. In cells D4 through D7 additional math actions are added to the linking function.

Linking can also be accomplished through Copy then Paste Special>Paste Link. When done with this method the references are created as Absolute References by Excel, the absolute reference function can be inserted on the "Look to" method as well. This allows the child cell to be moved, copied and pasted, or dragged to another location without losing its reference.

When Excel links between two workbooks the formula becomes slightly more complicated. The formula "=[Book3]Sheet1!$A$1" inserted into a cell in a workbook other than Book3 would look to Book3 and return the data entered in cell A1. In this formula the parent and child workbooks are within the same directory. If the source cell of a parent or source worksheet is updated while the dependent or child worksheet is not open, the dependent or child will ask if you want to update the linked value when it is opened the next time.

With the ability to link the worksheets and workbooks you can build subsidiary ledgers containing accounts receivable and accounts payable data and then link it to the general ledger of accounts receivable and accounts payable. The subsidiary ledgers would be the source or parent with the general ledger being the child or dependent cells. You would not have to have the general ledger open to make entries into the subsidiary ledgers but if, and when, changes are made to the subsidiary ledgers, Excel would ask if you would like the values to be updated upon opening the dependent or child general ledger.

Loan payments

Excel has numerous formulas that address loan payments. The most commonly used is the PMT formula. This formula is under the Financial category. With PMT you provide Excel with the period interest rate, the number of periods, the present value, the future value if any, and determine if the payment is made at the beginning or end of the period. The quickest way to access this formula is by clicking on the F_x of the formula entry window and ask for payment. Excel will present you with the Payment (PMT) dialog box which looks like this:

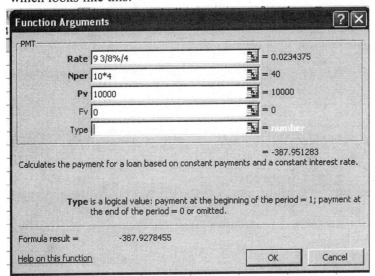

Excel requires the interest to be expressed in the same manner as the periods and the periods are determined by the compounding feature of the loan. If the interest rate is 12% annually but compounded monthly you can enter 12%/12 or 1%. The entry of 12%/12 would be considered safest since you do not have to do math outside the formula to determine values like 9 3/8% interest compounded quarterly, you can enter it as 9 3/8%/4 rather than calculate it out as 0.0234375 in decimal. Since the loan is a 10-year loan with quarterly payments you can enter 10*4 into the Nper or number of periods window. The principle amount is entered in the Pv window. As typical with Excel, no dollar signs or commas are appropriate. The Fv window is for future value, if the loan has a balloon payment, the value of that payment would be placed in this window. The Type window is where the schedule of payment, at the beginning or the end of the period, is established. The default is 0 (zero) and is assumed is not provided. With our loan data the dialog box is saying that our payment appears to be $387.95 per payment period. If we had made the principle amount a negative value the solution would be a positive value agreeing with the logic of a loan – if someone loans you money, the principle is a positive value or cash inflow to you while the payments are a negative value or cash outflow to you. Clicking on the OK button will post the formula to the worksheet. The completed formula inserted by Excel is =PMT(9.375%/4,10*4,10000,0). A review of this formula confirms our data entry. A quick check of the result, $387.95 X 40 payments indicates that we will be paying approximately $15,518 in payments. This value seems reasonable and can be checked with two other Excel formulas PPMT and IPMT. Examine the Loan tab of the chapter 9 data file to see an example of how a loan table can be constructed with these formulas.

Payment to principle

Payment to principle of a loan payment for a period can be determined by the PPMT formula or payment to principle formula. The data windows for this formula are very similar to the data entry windows for the PMT function detailed above except that PPMT asks for the period that you want the payment to principle for. This can be from period 1 to period 40 or any other period in the applicable range for our example. The output value is under the same logic as PMT – if the principle is positive, the payment will be negative. Examine the Loan tab of the chapter 9 data file to see an example of how a loan table can be constructed with these formulas. The formula CUMPRINC will generate the interest for a range of periods rather than one specific period with very little variance in its input values.

Payment to interest

The payment to interest of a loan payment for a period can be determined by the IPMT formula or payment to interest formula. The data windows for this formula are very similar to the data entry windows for the PMT function detailed above except that IPMT asks for the period that you want the payment to interest for. This can be from period 1 to period 40 or any other applicable range for our example. The output value is under the same logic as PMT – if the principle is positive, the payment will be negative. Examine the Loan tab of the chapter 9 data file to see an example of how a loan table can be constructed with these formulas.

The formula CUMIPMT will generate the interest for a range of periods rather than one specific period with very little variance in its input values.

EXERCISES

Exercise E9-2 (File 9e-2) Journalize entries to record allowance for doubtful accounts using two different methods

The ledger of Salizar Company at the end of the current year shows Accounts receivable of $110,000, Sales of $840,000, and Sales returns and allowances of $40,000.

Instructions:
(a) If Allowance for doubtful accounts has a credit balance of $2,500 in trial balance, journalize the adjusting entry at December 31, assuming bad debts are expected to be (1) 1% of net sales, and (2) 10% of accounts receivable.
(b) If Allowance for doubtful accounts has a debit balance of $500 in the trial balance, journalize the adjusting entry at December 31, assuming bad debts are expected to be (1) 0.75% of net sales, and (2) 6% of accounts receivable.

Exercise E9-11 (File 9e-11) Determine missing amounts related to sales and accounts receivable

The following information pertains to Moosa Merchandising Company:

Merchandise inventory at end of year	$33,000
Accounts receivable at beginning of year	24,000
Cash sales made during the year	15,000
Gross profit on sales	27,000
Accounts receivable written off during the year	1,000
Purchases made during the year	60,000
Accounts receivable collected during the year	78,000
Merchandise inventory at beginning of year	36,000

Instructions:

(a) Calculate the amount of credit sales made during the year. (*Hint:* You will need to use income statement relationships – introduced in Chapter 5 of the text book – in order to determine this.)

(b) Calculate the balance of accounts receivable at the end of the year.

PROBLEMS

Problem P9-1A (File 9p-1a) Prepare journal entries related to bad debt expense

At December 31, 2002, Cellular Ten Co. reported the following information on its balance sheet:

Accounts receivable	$960,000
Less: Allowance for doubtful accounts	70,000

During 2003, the company had the following transactions related to receivables:

1	Sales on account	$3,300,000
2	Sales returns and allowances	50,000
3	Collections of accounts receivable	2,800,000
4	Write-offs of accounts receivable deemed uncollectible	90,000
5	Recovery of bad debts previously written off as uncollectible	25,000

Instructions:

(a) Prepare the journal entries to record each of these five transactions. Assuming that no cash discounts were taken on the collections of accounts receivable.

(b) Enter the January 1, 2003, balances in Accounts receivable and Allowance for doubtful accounts, post the entries to the two accounts (use T accounts), and determine the balances.

(c) Prepare the journal entry to record bad debts expense for 2003, assuming that an aging of accounts receivable indicates that expected bad debts are $125,000.

(d) Compute the accounts receivable turnover ratio for 2003.

Problem P9-6A (File 9p-6a) Prepare entries for various receivables transactions

On January 1, 2002, John Diego Company had Accounts receivable of $146,000, Notes receivable of $15,000, and Allowance for doubtful accounts of $13,200. The note receivable is from Trudy Borke Company. It is a 4-month, 12% note dated December 31, 2001. John Diego Company prepares financial statements annually. During the year the following selected transactions occurred:

Jan 5   Sold $18,000 of merchandise to Jones Company, terms net 15.

Jan 20   Accepted Jones Company's $18,000, 3-month, 9% note for balance due.

Feb 18   Sold $8,000 of merchandise to Swan Company and accepted Swan's $8,000, 6-month, 10% note for the amount due.

Apr 20   Collected Jones Company note in full.

Apr 30   Received payment in full from Trudy Borke Company on the amount due.

May 25 Accepted Avita Inc., $6,000, 3-month, 8% note in settlement of a past due balance on account.

Aug 18   Received payment in full from Swan Company on note due.

Aug 25   The Avita Inc. note was dishonored. Avita Inc. is not bankrupt; future payment is anticipated.

Sep 1   Sold $12,000 of merchandise to Jose Trevino Company and accepted a $12,000, 6-month, 10% note for the amount due.

Instructions:

Journalize the transactions.

CHAPTER 10

PLANT ASSETS, NATURAL RESOURCES, AND INTANGIBLE ASSETS

CLUES, HINTS, AND TIPS

Asset acquisition summary sheet

The acquisition of a plant, property, equipment, intangible, or natural resource asset is seldom a simple one page document event. Take for example the acquisition of a land plot, the construction of a new plant building, and the purchase of equipment for the plant. The land may have purchase price, commissions, back taxes, current taxes, survey costs, title searches, title insurance, and court and filing fees associated with it. The construction of the plant may have survey costs, architectural and design costs, environmental impact statement costs, construction fees, insurance during construction, interest and finance fees incurred during and after construction, legal fees, filing fees, and bonding fees. The purchase of a piece of major equipment for the new plant may have purchase price, commissions, site surveys, transportation, insurance during transportation and installation, installation costs, bonding of installation contractor, licensing and certification costs, costs for test materials, costs of training materials and labor while training line personnel and other costs. Not all of these costs may be contributable to the asset depreciable cost. Excel can assist you in documenting the costs and the location of the source documents associated with the acquisition. You can create a generic template within Excel with the various costs that might be involved and identify those costs as acquisition costs, depreciable costs, period costs, or any other category you may feel is appropriate. By including columns for items such as to whom the value was paid and where the source documents are filed the sheet can be a great aid when inserted into the asset's file. Here is an example of a possible acquisition summary sheet for a land plot:

Asset:	Land plot at 3rd and B Streets			Date:	January 2, 2000
Item:	Amount:	Classification:	Paid to:		Document location:
Purchase price	$75,000	Acquisition	Mrs. J.K. Conners		3rd & B St file
Commissions	$3,750	Acquisition	Valley Realty		3rd & B St file
Back taxes	$4,200	Acquisition	San Diego County		SD Cty Tax file
Current taxes	$1,250	Period	San Diego County		SD Cty Tax file
Title search	$750	Acquisition	County Title Svc		3rd & B St file
Title insurance	$1,500	Acquisition	State Title Insurance		3rd & B St file
Survey costs	$2,000	Acquisition	Inland Survey Svc		3rd & B St file
Filing fee	$45	Acquisition	San Diego County		SD Cty Tax file
Prepaid interest	$425	Period	Lenders Banking Ltd		Lenders Banking
Acquisition costs:	$87,245				
Period costs:	$1,675				
Total:	$88,920				

Straight-line depreciation

The straight-line depreciation concept is handled through the SLN formula of Excel. This formula is shown in use in the chapter 10 data file, chptr10, on the Straight-line tab. The example takes advantage of absolute references and embedded formulas to generate the period expense per month for the life of the asset, the book value of the asset at each month through the asset's life, and the accumulated depreciation through the monthly periods of the asset's life. The straight-line depreciation formula of Excel is found under the financial category and requires asset cost, asset salvage value, and life. The life must be in the same factor or terms that you wish to record the depreciation in. If you record depreciation monthly, state the life in months, if you record depreciation quarterly, state the life in quarters, if you record depreciation annually, state the life in years. For an asset with a cost of $2,400, a salvage value of $300, and a life of 120 months, the formula is =SLN(2400,300,120). Because straight-line depreciation is simple math the formula can be manually entered as =(2400-300)/120. Both will result in approximately $17.50 per month. Because the example on the data file uses cell references, the formula read on cell C7 is =SLN($B$2,$B$3,$B$4). The $B$2 refers to the cell with asset cost in it, the $B$3 refers to the cell with the salvage value in it, the $B$4 refers to the cell with the life factor in it.

Declining-balance depreciation

Excel handles declining balance depreciation through the DDB formula found in the financial category. The formula requires asset cost, asset salvage value, life, period of life, and depreciation factor. Excel expects the number 2 or the percentage 200% to represent double-declining depreciation. Excel will accept and work with any schedule entered in these formats. Depreciation at 150% declining balance would be input as 1.5 or 150%

The chapter 10 data file shows the formula in action with the same basic values as utilized for the straight-line depreciation above. The formula is =DDB($B$2,$B$3,$B$4,A7,$B$5) or =DDB(2400,300,120,period of life cell reference, factor). The period of life cell reference is required because the amount of period depreciation is controlled by the balance at the beginning of that particular period. The factor will default to 2 or 200% if left blank.

Notice that the DDB formula works well for short runs but longer periods may require an adjustment at the end of the life of the asset to get the asset to fully depreciated amount. If the life of the asset is changed to 10 on the DDB tab, the depreciation is exactly $2,100 for the life of the asset with an ending book value of $300. If the life of the asset is set to 120 the book value at the end of the depreciable life is approximately $319 with accumulated depreciation of approximately $2,080 so the last period depreciation would have to be adjusted to get it to exactly $300 book value with total depreciation of $2,100 over the life time of the asset. This type of adjustment is not uncommon with accelerated deprecation schedules.

Declining balance to straight-line depreciation

Excel will handle the concept of accelerated depreciation at the outset of the schedule and then converting to straight-line when it becomes beneficial. This is accomplished through the VDB formula or Variable Declining Balance. Like the DDB formula it requires cost, salvage value, life, period reference and factor. VDB also requires a specific statement if you want to switch to straight-line or retain accelerated depreciation throughout the schedule. By inserting a 0 (zero) into the No Switch window, Excel will maintain accelerated depreciation through the life of the asset, by inserting a 1 (one), Excel will switch to straight-line when it provides a greater benefit (more depreciation in the period) than continued accelerated depreciation. The chapter 10 data file, chptr10 shows this formula in action on the VDB tab. The formula to reference the cells is =VDB($B$2,$B$3,$B$4,0,A7,$B$5,1).

One item of note on this formula is that for the first period's depreciation to be correct, the start period must be set to 0 (zero) and the end period would be set to 1, or as in the formula, it references the period number column. Once dragged into the second period the formula has to be retouched to start at the period above the row the formula is on and to end on the formula's row number. This will give the period depreciation. This formula is capable of generating the depreciation for more than one period through the start and end period windows. Because of the conversion to straight-line near the end of the depreciable life, there is seldom any adjustment needed at the end of the depreciation cycle as with DDB.

Sum-of-year's-digits depreciation

Excel handles Sum-of-year's digits depreciation through the SYD formula. On the SYD tab of the chapter 10 data file, chptr10, you will see this formula in action. The sum-of-year's digits formula requires the same information as previously provided to the DDB and VDB formulas with the exception of the factor. With the SYD formula however, it is recommended that you remain with years as life and divide the annual amount of depreciation by 12 if you are posting depreciation monthly or divide annual depreciation by 4 if posting depreciation quarterly.

The formula for Sum-of-year's digits depreciation is =SYD($B$2,$B$3,$B$4,A7) where $B$2 refers to the asset cost, $B$3 refers to the salvage value, $B$4 refers to the life in years, and A7 refers to the year of the calculation.

Units of activity

Excel does not have a formula to handle Units of activity depreciation. While the concept is rather simple, the sum of acquisition cost less salvage value divided by the expected units, an Excel formula to handle it gets rather complicated if it is written to provide period depreciation, calculate book value, and calculate accumulated depreciation without violating the concepts of depreciation. The chapter 10 data file has a working model of how this function can be written into Excel on the Units of Activity tab. This model makes extensive use of embedded formulas to ensure that depreciable amount is not exceeded either in total or in period entry. Examination of the formulas in rows 7 and 8 of column D will show that the initial formula in line 7 is not appropriate for the lines below line 7. Column D, line 7 needs to ensure that the single event of that period's activity does not exceed the depreciable amount, if it does, it needs to calculate the maximum depreciable amount and enter it, if it does not exceed the maximum depreciable amount, it needs to calculate the period depreciation based on the cost, salvage value, and expected units. In row 8 and below, the formula needs to determine the amount of depreciation already taken and if that amount equals the maximum amount allowable, it needs to preclude depreciation in this period. Then the formula needs to determine if this period's activities added to the previous periods activities will exceed the maximum amount of depreciation allowable, if so, what is the appropriate amount of depreciation applicable to the period? Lastly, the formula calculates the period depreciation based on cost, salvage value, expected total units of activity and actual activity if no violations or limitations are calculated. Then columns E and F track book value and accumulated depreciation.

Notice the extensive use of the "If", sum, and absolute references within these formulas. Review the section on embedded formulas if necessary. Notice that the only equal sign in the formula is the beginning character.

EXERCISES

Exercise E10-3 (File 10e-3) Compute depreciation under units-of-activity method

Always Late Bus Lines uses the units-of-activity method in depreciating its buses. One bus was purchased on January 1, 2002 at a cost of $128,000. Over its 4-year useful life, the bus is expected to be driven 100,000 miles. Salvage value is expected to be $8,000.

Instructions:
(a) Compute the depreciation cost per unit.
(b) Prepare a depreciation schedule assuming actual mileage was:

Year 2002	26,000
Year 2003	32,000
Year 2004	25,000
Year 2005	17,000

Exercise E10-6 (File 10e-6) Journalize entries for disposal of plant assets

Presented below are selected transactions at Beck Company for 2002:

Jan 1   Retired a piece of machinery that was purchased on January 1, 1992. The machine cost $62,000 on that date. It had a useful life of 10 years with no salvage value.

Jun 30   Sold a computer that was purchased on January 1, 1999. The computer cost $35,000. It had a useful life of 7 years with no salvage value. The computer was sold for $22,000.

Dec 31   Discarded a delivery truck that was purchased on January 1, 1998. The truck cost $30,000. It was depreciated based on a 6-year useful life with a $3,000 salvage value.

Instructions:

Journalize all entries required on the above dates, including entries to update depreciation, where applicable, on assets disposed of. Beck Company uses straight-line depreciation. (Assume depreciation is up to date as of December 31, 2001.)

PROBLEMS

Problem P10-2A (File 10p-2a) Compute depreciation under different methods

In recent years, Waterfront Transportation purchased three used buses. Because of frequent turnover in the accounting department, a different accountant selected the depreciation method for each bus, and various methods were selected. Information concerning the buses is summarized below:

Bus	Acquired	Cost	Salvage value	Useful life	Deprecation method
1	1/1/2000	$86,000	$6,000	4 years	Straight-line
2	1/1/2000	140,000	10,000	5 years	Declining balance
3	1/1/2001	80,000	8,000	5 years	Units-of-activity

For the declining balance method, the company uses the double-declining rate. For the units-of-activity method, total miles are expected to be 120,000. Actual miles of use in the first three years were:

2001	24,000
2002	3,400
2003	30,000

Instructions:

(a) Compute the amount of accumulated depreciation on each bus at December 31, 2002.

(b) If bus No. 2 was purchased on April 1 instead of January 1, what is the depreciation expense for this bus in (1) 2000 and (2) 2001?

Problem P10-8A (File 10p-8a) Prepare entries to correct for errors made in recording and amortizing intangible assets

Due to rapid turnover in the accounting department, a number of transactions involving intangible assets were improperly recorded by the Henry Company in 2002.

1. Henry developed a new manufacturing process, incurring research and development costs of $186,900. The company also purchased a patent for $39,100. In early January, Henry capitalized $226,000 as the cost of the patents. Patent amortization expense of $11,300 was recorded on a 20-year useful life.

2. On July 1, 2002, Henry purchased a small company and as a result acquired goodwill of $92,000. Henry recorded a half-year's amortization in 2002, based on a 50-year life ($920 amortization).

Instructions:

Prepare all journal entries necessary to correct any errors made during 2002. Assume the books have not yet been closed for 2002.

CHAPTER 11

LIABILITIES

CLUES, HINTS, AND TIPS

Present Value

Excel has a very powerful and easy to utilize formula for present value calculations under the title of PV in the financial category. This single formula will handle present value calculations of single sums or annuities as well as adjust them for payment at the beginning or the end of the period. The inserted screen print shows the Present Value dialog box. The chapter 11 data file, chptr11, has numerous examples on the Present Value tab. The basic formula is =PV(Period interest, Number of periods, Amount of each payments, Future value, Payment at the beginning or the end of the period) with payment at the end of the period indicated by a 0 (zero) and payment at the beginning of the period indicated by a 1 (one). Leaving the payment type empty Excel defaults to payment at the end of the period. By omitting the value for payments or by placing a 0 (zero) in the window and providing the formula a future value, the formula

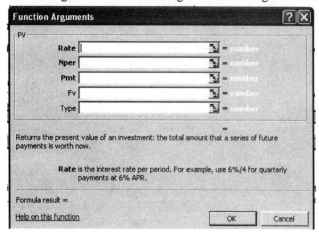

will produce the present value of a single sum. By placing the amount of an individual payment in the payment window the formula will produce the present value of an annuity. For annuities due place a 1 (one) in the Type window, for an ordinary annuity, place a 0 (zero) in the Type window or leave it blank.

Some hints and tips on utilizing the dialog box – First, if you establish the data matrix as shown on the Present Value tab in cells A1 through D7 you can have formulas installed that will take the life in years and multiply it by the compounding factor for Nper. You can also divide the interest rate by the compounding factor to get the value for the period rate. Remember that as with working with the tables in the text book, the interest rate and the number of periods must be expressed in comparable values. If the document states that interest is 8% annually and it is compounded quarterly and that the life of the annuity is 10 years, the effective values are 2% interest (8% / 4 quarters) and 40 periods (10 years X 4 quarters per year).

The formula will also produce the value of $1, just like the tables by placing the value of 1 (one) in the payment or future value window as appropriate. This value will be carried out to more significant digits than the text book's tables even if formatted to show the same since Excel keeps the real value in its "mind" even with trimmed or formatted presentations.

Excel works with standard finance and math logic. If the payments are positive, the present value will be negative, if the payments are negative, the present value is positive. This represents cash flows in and out with cash flows out being negatives and cash flows in being positives.

Future Value

Excel has a similar formula for Future value as it as for Present value under the Financial category. This formula is demonstrated on the Future value tab of the chapter 11 data file, chptr11. The formula is written as =FV(Period Interest, Periods, Payments, Future value, Payment at the beginning or the end of the period). As with the present value formula interest rate and periods must be stated in the same terms. The appearance of the dialog box is very similar. Like the present value formula this single formula with various inputs will provide the future value of a single sum or a series of payments, an annuity. It will accept payments made at the beginning or the end of the period. As with the present value formula the future value formula will produce the value for the sum of $1. This value will be kept within Excel to a greater number of significant digits than your text book's tables. This may cause a slight difference between Excel generated present and future values but the differences will not be material.

Bond tables

Excel will handle the task of a bond issuance, determination of present value of the issue and both effective and straight-line amortization of the premium or discount. As stated in the text book, the essential pieces of information for a bond issuance are face interest rate, market interest rate, periodicity of bond interest payments, life of the bond, number of bonds issued and the face value of each bond as well as whether the amortization will be effective or straight-line amortization. By using the PV formula of Excel you can determine the present value of the principle and the present value of the interest payments. The sum of these two values is the present value of the issuance. The difference between the present value of the issuance and the face value of the issuance determines whether the bond was issued at a premium or discount and the amount of that premium or discount. With the power of worksheets available on the desktop system effective interest amortization computation is almost as easy as straight-line amortization – except that because of the varying amount per period for effective interest method the journal entry cannot effectively be memorized.

There is a bond table contained in the chapter 11 data file, chptr11, on the tab Premium - Discount. The top 14 rows of this tab contains live formulas and will generate the present value of the bonds as well as determine if the bond is being issued at a premium or a discount and compute the amount of the premium or discount. The remainder of the formulas have been removed through Copy and then Paste Special > Values. A second copy is placed on the Working tab. On the Working tab you are provided with same data as on the Premium – Discount tab. You can use the worksheet on this tab as a starting point to complete the bond table. To the right of the effective interest rate amortization method is a straight-line amortization method so the difference can be evaluated. Both tables use the same data. The table became static with face interest rate of 7% and a market interest rate of 6%.

EXERCISES

Exercise E11-1 (File 11e-1) Prepare entries for interest bearing notes

Nicolas Cage Company on June 1 borrows $50,000 from Corner Bank on a 6-month $50,000, 12% note.

Instructions:
(a) Prepare the entry for June 1.
(b) Prepare the adjusting entry on June 30.
(c) Prepare the entry at maturity (December 1), assuming monthly adjusting entries have been made through November 30.
(d) What was the total financing cost (interest expense)?

Exercise E11-5 (File 11e-5) Prepare entries for the issuance bonds and payment of accrual of bond interest

On January 1, Penelope Cruz Company issued $90,000, 10%, 10-year bonds at face value. Interest is payable semiannually on July 1 and January 1. Interest is not accrued on June 30.

Instructions:
Present journal entries to record the following:
(a) The issuance of the bonds.
(b) The payment of interest on July 1.
(c) The accrual of interest on December 31.

Exercise E11-7 (File 11e-7) Prepare entries to record issuance of bonds, payment of interest, amortization of discount, and redemption at maturity

Torilla Company issues $180,000, 11%, 10-year bonds on December 31, 2002, for $172,000. Interest is payable semiannually on June 30 and December 31. Torilla uses the straight-line method to amortize bond premium or discount.

Instructions:
Prepare the journal entries to record the following:
   (a) The issuance of the bonds.
   (b) The payment of interest and the discount amortization on June 30, 2003.
   (c) The payment of interest and discount amortization on December 31, 2003.
   (d) The redemption of bonds at maturity, assuming interest for the last interest period has been paid and recorded.

PROBLEMS

Problem P11-2A (File 11p-2a) Journalize and post note transactions and show balance sheet presentation

The following are selected transactions of Detroit Company. Detroit prepares financial statements *quarterly*. (A perpetual inventory system is used.)

Jan 2   Purchased merchandise on account from Teresa Speck Company, $15,000, terms 2/10, net 30.

Feb 1   Issued a 10%, 2-month, $15,000 note to Teresa Speck Company in payment of account.

Mar 31 Accrued interest for 2 months on Teresa Speck Company note.

Apr 1   Paid face value and interest on Teresa Speck Company note.

July 1   Purchased equipment from Scottie Equipment paying $11,000 in cash and signing a 10%, 3-month, $24,000 note.

Sep 30 Accrued interest for 3 months on Scottie Equipment note.

Oct 1   Paid face value and interest on Scottie Equipment note.

Dec 1   Borrowed $10,000 from Federation Bank by issuing a 3-month, 9% interest-bearing note with a face value of $10,000.

Dec 31 Recognized interest expense for 1 month on Federation Bank note.

Instructions:
(a) Prepare journal entries for the above transactions and events.
(b) Post to the accounts Notes payable, Interest payable, and Interest expense.
(c) Show the balance sheet presentation of notes payable at December 31.
(d) What is the total interest expense for the year.

Problem P11-5A (File 11p-5a) Prepare entries to record interest payments, discount amortization, and redemption of bonds

The following data is taken from the Hernandez Corp. balance sheet:

HERNANDEZ CORP
Balance Sheet (Partial)
December 31, 2002

Current liabilities		
Bond interest payable (for 6 months from Jul 1 to Dec 31)		$132,000
Long-term liabilities		
Bonds payable, 11%, due Jan 1, 2013	$2,400,000	
Less: Discount on bonds payable	84,000	$2,316,000

Interest is payable semiannually on January 1 and July 1. The bonds are callable on any semiannual interest date. Hernandez uses straight-line amortization for any bond premium or discount. From December 31, 2002, the bonds will be outstanding for an additional 10 years or 120 months. Assume no interest is accrued on June 30.

Instructions:
(Round all computations to the nearest dollar.)
(a) Journalize the payment of bond interest on January 1, 2003.
(b) Prepare the journal entry to amortize bond discount and to pay the interest due on July 1, 2003.
(c) Assume on July 1, 2003, after paying interest that Hernandez Corp calls bonds having a face value of $800,000. The call price is 102. Record the redemption of the bonds.
(d) Prepare the adjusting entry at December 31, 2003, to amortize bond discount and to accrue interest on the remaining bonds.

Problem P11-8A (File 11p-8a) Prepare entries to record issuance of bonds, payment of interest, and amortization of premium using effective interest method, answer questions

On July 1, 2002, Imperial Oil Company issued $2,000,000 face value, 12%, 10-year bonds at $2,249,245. This price resulted in a 10% effective-interest rate on the bonds. Imperial Oil uses the effective-interest method to amortize bond premium or discount. The bonds pay semiannual interest on each July 1 and January 1.

Instructions:
(a) Prepare the journal entries to record the following transactions:
  (1) The issuance of the bonds on July 1, 2002.
  (2) The accrual of interest and the amortization of the premium on December 31, 2002.
  (3) The payment of interest and the amortization of premium on July 1, 2003.
  (4) The accrual of interest and the amortization of the premium on December 31, 2003.
(b) Show the proper balance sheet presentation for the liability for bonds payable on the December 31, 2003 balance sheet date.
(c) Provide the answers to the following questions in letter form, addressed to the comptroller of Imperial Oil:
  (1) What amount of interest expense is reported for 2003?
  (2) Would the bond interest reported in 2003 be the same as, greater than, or less than the amount

that would be reported if the straight-line method of amortization were used?
(3) Determine the total cost of borrowing over the life of the bond.
(4) Would the total bond interest expense be greater than, the same as, or less than the total interest expense if the straight-line method of amortization were used?

Problem P11-2B (File 11p-2b) Prepare entries for the issuance bonds, interest accrual, and amortization for 2 years

Joffrey Ballet Corp. sold $3,000,000, 10%, 10-year bonds on January 1, 2002. The bonds were dated January 1 and pay interest July 1 and January 1. Joffrey Ballet Corp. uses the straight-line method to amortize bond premium or discount. The bonds were sold at 104. Assume no interest is accrued on June 30.

Instructions:
(a) Prepare the journal entry to record the issuance of the bonds on January 1, 2002.
(b) Prepare a bond premium amortization schedule for the first four interest periods.
(c) Prepare the journal entries for interest and the amortization of the premium in 2002 and 2003.
(d) Show the balance sheet presentation of the bond liability at December 31, 2003.

Problem P11-4B (File 11p-4b) Prepare entries to record issuance of bonds, interest, and amortization of bond premium and discount

Chula Vista Corporation sold $3,500,000, 7%, 20-year bonds on June 30, 2002. The bonds were dated June 30, 2002 and pay interest on June 30 and December 31. The company uses straight-line amortization for bond premiums and discounts. Financial statements are prepared annually.

Instructions:
(a) Prepare the journal entry to record the issuance of the bonds assuming they are sold at:
   (1) 96 ½
   (2) 104
(b) Prepare amortization tables for both the assumed sales for the first three interest payments.
(c) Prepare the journal entries to record the first two interest payments under assumed sales.
(d) Show the balance sheet presentation for both assumed sales at December 31, 2002.

CHAPTER 12

CORPORATIONS: ORGANIZATION, STOCK TRANSACTIONS, DIVIDENDS, AND RETAINED EARNINGS

CHAPTER OUTLINE

CLUES, HINTS, AND TIPS

Audit

Excel as a very useful aid for assisting you with the checks of your formulas and logic. The Audit function is controlled through the Audit tool bar or menu. To display this tool bar, right click on the menu bars at the top of the Excel screen, from the pop-up menu select the Formula Auditing option, highlighted to the left, from the options. When this tool bar appears place and hold your cursor over the various icons and Windows will display the function of the icon. The icons of primary interest are Trace Precedents and Trace Dependent. Click into cell C3 of the Audit tab on the chapter 12 data file, chptr12 and make cell C3 the active cell. Then click on the icon for Trace precedents and Excel will display arrows from the all of

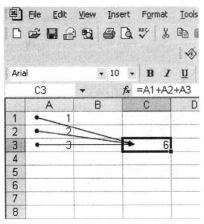

the cells that feed this cell data. This is shown on the screen print. If the source cell is a formula, Excel will not "trace through" to that cell's source. To be effective, the Trace precedents must be activated from a cell with a formula that references at least one other cell. To remove the audit arrows you can click the eraser on the tool bar and all audit arrows will disappear, regardless of where your active cell is. To make only one cell's audit arrows disappear, click into that cell and click the icon with the negative signs for the action – dependent or precedent.

Click into cell C1. While cell C1 is the active cell, click on the Trace dependent icon on the formula auditing tool bar. A single arrow will appear from cell A1 to cell C3, pointing at cell C3 showing that the data flow is from cell A1 to cell C3. To see that cell A3 is also a source cell for cell C3 you can either click into cell A3 and click onto the Trace dependent icon or click into cell C3 and click on the Trace precedents icon. Once again, the trace icons with negative signs make individual arrows go away, the eraser on the tool bar makes them all go way.

You can also access the Audit tools through the path Tools>Formula Auditing from the main menu bar. With this path you can select a single event or elect to display the tool bar.

Find

With Excel worksheets being as large as they can be and the display screen as small as it is, it is often hard to find a specific item quickly. Particularly if a prankster has hidden it by changing its font to white on a white background filled cell. There are four hidden text strings on the Audit tab of the data file for chapter 12. Two cells have the value "Hi!!!!" and two cells have the value "You found it!!!!" in them. By using the key strokes Ctrl-F (for find) or following the path Edit>Find you will be given the Excel Find dialog box. In the Find what window enter "Hi" – without the quotation marks or one or more but less than 5 exclamation points (!). When Find Now or Find All is clicked, Excel will initiate the search and find one of the two strings. The cell that Excel locates will contain no visible text since the text coloring and the cell background are both white. However, in the formula window you will read "Hi!!!!".

At this point, close the dialog box. When the dialog box is closed, look at the borders of the cell just below the cell that contains the "Hi!!!!". Something is causing the right side of that cell not to display properly. By clicking into the cell you will find the first of the "You found it!!!!" text strings. Click into a cell 3~5 cells above these two cells and then highlight the cells in the column down about 10 rows and 2 or 3 columns to the right. You will see the text strings appear in the blue highlight as white text. Hint – looking for something hidden and do not know where it is? Try highlighting the cells. Excel will tell you about how much of the worksheet has been used by the scroll bars. The more the scroll bars can move, the larger the worksheet data range. Continue into the next section, Protection to find the next two text strings. This subject is continued in Protection and Find and Replace because of its interactions.

Tip – If a range of cells is highlighted when the Find function is activated, it will only search those cells. Excel will frequently ask if you want to search the rest of the worksheet but there are instances where you do not get that advisor because you closed the function prior to the function completing the find on the selected cells.

Protection

You are still unable to locate the second set of test strings even with Excel's Find function. Clue – under formatting functions of cells you can protect and hide cells. When a cell is formatted under the protection tab of cell formatting with the features of hidden and locked and protection is empowered through the path >Tools>Protection>Protect worksheet, Excel will not reveal the data during find or find and replace. Scroll through the cells in the range of X560 through Z580 to look for telltale signs like the irregular cell borders. Check to see if the worksheet has protection active by following the path Tools>Protection. If the option is "Unprotect worksheet" the protection feature is active. Simply click the option and protection will be removed if no password has been utilized. This command is a toggle – click once and it is on, click again and it is off. Look at the range X560 through Z580 for irregularities. Now that the protection is off try the find function for "You found it!!!!". This time Excel should find two cells. If you selected the find now function, Excel found one cell and then you were required to click find next. If you clicked Find all, Excel identified all of the cells in a dialog box. By clicking on either of the located cells, Excel will take you to that cell.

When protection is active on the worksheet Excel will not expose cells with this function active upon them. Excel will not reveal the contents in the formula window, it will not expose the possible presence by presenting irregular borders.

To protect a worksheet follow the path Tools>Protection and select Protect worksheet. When you make that selection Excel will present you with a pop-up dialog box asking what parameters you wish to invoke and if you want a password. If you utilize a password, beware, the worksheet may be very hard to open if you forget it. Since the default cell value for Excel is "Locked", protecting a worksheet will allow others to view but not change it – unless other protection options are selected.

Find and Replace

Excel has another Find function, this one associated with an added option of Replace. This function is activated by the key strokes Ctrl-H, by following the path Edit>Find and Replace, or by selecting Options on the Find function. The find and replace function is powerful (and dangerous).

Tip – One of the safest ways to control Find and Replace is to limit its range by selecting a column, a row, a cell, or a range of cells rather than letting it roam the worksheet. The second safest thing (no in any order) is to utilize the Find next button and then determine if you want the next item found replaces. If you do, click the replace button and Excel will replace that one item and then find the next one. If you do not want that one item replaced, click the Find next button and Excel will move on without replacing it.

The Find and Replace tab of the chapter 12 data file, chptr12, contains a minor exercise in Find and Replace. Open up the data file and click into cells C5 and D5 of the Find and Replace tab. This range selection will contain Excel's find and replace powers to two cells for the demonstration. Use the key strokes Ctrl-H to bring up the Find and Replace dialog box. Since you want the formula to be absolute referenced so you can move it elsewhere without changing its relational reference, tell Excel to find the letter A in the Find what window, upper or lower case does not matter. In the Replace with window tell Excel to replace it with A. This will remove the relational A column reference and replace it with an absolute column reference and at the same time make the row reference absolute without having to do find and replace on every number – which is dangerous because if told to replace 5 with $5, 55 will become $5$5, which will generate an error. Now click on Replace All and Excel will replace about 6 A's and convert the relational formula an absolute formula that can be dragged anywhere without losing its references to the three ranges in column A.

Now click the select all button above the row 1 indicator and to the left of the column A indicator. Once the worksheet is highlighted, bring up the find and replace dialog box and instruct Excel to replace the letter A with the number 4 and then click Replace all on the command buttons. Excel will stop and give you an error message since the insertion of the number 4 into the formulas will cause an error and Excel will allow you to type enter the error but it will not commit it on its own. Click the OK on the error box and click Find next on the find and replace dialog box. When Excel finds the text strings tell it to replace the characters. Excel has no problems making nonsense text strings because it cannot "read" English. Now tell Excel to find and replace all of the A's with the letter B. Excel will change every formula on the page since this will not commit a formula error.

Excel's Find and Replace is powerful and quite useful. Tip – use your imagination to control it or your results may not be what is expected.

Indent within a cell

To indent within a cell without using spaces use the Indent icon on the tool bar. Each click on the icon moves the start of text and numerical data about 2 spaces. Remember that by default text is left justified and numerical data is right justified. Asking Excel to indent numerical data to the right in a default formatted cell will not result in a move nor will asking Excel to indent text data to the left in a in default formatted cell. However, if the contents of the cell have been indented one way, clicking on the other ident icon will result in a shift. Many of the cells within the templates have indented cells since this is not removed with the contents of the cells are removed or typed over.

EXERCISES

Exercise E12-2 (File 12e-2) Prepare entries for issuance of common and preferred stock and the purchase of treasury stock

Phoenix Co. had the following transactions during the current period:
  Mar 2   Issued 5,000 shares of $1 par value common stock to attorneys in payment of a bill for $27,000 for services rendered in helping the company to incorporate.
  Jun 12 Issued 60,000 shares of $1 par value common stock for cash of $375,000.
  Jul 11 Issued 1,000 shares of $100 par value preferred stock for cash at $105 per share.
  Nov 28 Purchased 2,000 shares of treasury stock for $80,000.

Instructions:
Journalize the transactions.

Exercise E12-9 (File 12e-9) Journalize stock dividends

On January 1, 2002, Tanner Tucci Corporation had $1,500,000 of common stock outstanding that was issued at par, and retained earnings of $750,000. The company issued $50,000 shares of common stock at par on July 1 and earned net income of $400,000 for the year.

Instructions:
Journalize the declaration of a 10% stock dividend on December 10, 2002, for the following independent assumptions:
  (1) Par value is $10 and market value is $15.
  (2) Par value is $5 and market value is $20.

PROBLEMS

Problem P12-1A (File 12p-1a) Journalize stock transactions, post, and prepare paid-in capital section

East Aurora Corporation was organized on January 1, 2002. It is authorized to issue 10,000 shares of 8%, $100 par value preferred stock, and 500,000 shares of no-par common stock with a stated value of $2 per share. The following stock transactions were completed during the first year:
  Jan 10 Issued 80,000 shares of common stock for cash at $3 per share.
  Mar 1   Issued 5,000 shares of preferred stock for cash at $104 per share.
  Apr 1   Issued 24,000 shares of common stock for land. The asking price of the land was $90,000. The fair value of the land was $80,000.
  May 1   Issued 80,000 shares of common stock at $4 per share.
  Aug 1   Issued 10,000 shares of common stock to attorneys in payment of their bill of $50,000 for services rendered in helping the company organize.
  Sep 1   Issued 10,000 shares of common stock for cash at $5 per share.
  Nov 1   Issued 1,000 shares of preferred stock for cash at $108 per share.

Instructions:
(a) Journalize the transactions.
(b) Post to the stockholders' equity accounts. (Use J5 as the posting reference.)
(c) Prepare the paid-in capital section of stockholders' equity at December 31, 2002.

Problem P12-6A (File 12p-6a) Prepare retained earnings statement and stockholders' equity section

The post-closing trial balance of Malaysia Corporation at December 31, 2002, contains the following stockholders' equity accounts:

Preferred stock (15,000 shares issued)	$750,000
Common stock(250,000 shares issued)	2,500,000
Paid-in capital in excess of par value - P/S	250,000

Paid-in capital in excess of par value - C/S	500,000
Common stock dividends distributable	200,000
Retained earnings	743,000

A review of the accounting records reveals the following:

1. No errors have been made in recording 2002 transactions or in preparing the closing entry for net income.
2. Preferred stock is $50 par, 10% cumulative, 15,000 shares have been outstanding since January 1, 2001.
3. Authorized stock is 20,000 shares of preferred, 500,000 shares of common stock with a $10 par value.
4. The January 1 balance in Retained earnings was $920,000.
5. On July 1, 20,000 shares of common stock were sold for cash at $16 per share.
6. On September 1, the company discovered an understatement error of $60,000 in computing depreciation in 2001. The net of tax effect of $42,000 was properly debited directly to Retained earnings.
7. A cash dividend of $250,000 was declared and properly allocated to preferred and common stock on October 1. No dividends were paid to preferred stockholders in 2001.
8. On December 31, an 8% common stock dividend was declared out of retained earnings on common stock when the market price per share was $16.
9. Net income for the year was $435,000.
10. On December 31, 2002, the directors authorized disclosure of a $200,000 restriction of retained earnings for plant expansion. (Use Note X.)

Instructions:
(a) Reproduce the retained earnings account for the year 2002.
(b) Prepare a retained earnings statement for the year 2002.
(c) Prepare a stockholders' equity section at December 31, 2002.

Problem P12-3B (File 12p-3b) Journalize and post transactions; prepare stockholders' equity section; compute book value

The stockholders' equity accounts of Pedro Corporation on January 1, 2002, were as follows:

Preferred stock (10%, $100 par noncumulative, 5,000 shares authorized)	$300,000
Common stock($5 stated value, 300,000 shares authorized)	1,000,000
Paid-in capital in excess of par value - P/S	15,000
Paid-in capital in excess of par value - C/S	400,000
Retained earnings	488,000
Treasury stock (5,000 shares)	40,000

During 2002, the corporation had the following transactions and events pertaining to its stockholders' equity:

Feb 1   Issued 4,000 shares of common stock for $250,000.
Mar 20 Purchased 1,000 additional shares of common treasury stock at $8 per share.
Jun 14 Sold 4,000 shares of treasury stock – common for $34,000.
Sept 3 Issued 2,000 shares of common stock for a patent valued at $13,000.
Dec 31 Determined that net income for the year was $215,000.

Instructions:
(a) Journalize the transactions and the closing entry for net income.
(b) Enter the beginning balances in the accounts and post the journal entries to the stockholders' equity accounts. (Use J1 as the posting reference.)
(c) Prepare a stockholders' equity section of the balance sheet at December 31, 2002.
(d) Compute the book value per share of common stock at December 31, 2002, assuming the preferred stock does not have a call price.

Problem P12-4B (File 12p-4b) Prepare retained earnings statement and the stockholders' equity sections

On December 31, 2002, Norway Company had 1,500,000 shares of $10 par common stock issued and outstanding. The stockholders' equity accounts at December 31, 2001, had the following balances:

Common stock	$15,000,000
Additional paid-in capital - C/S	1,500,000
Retained earnings	900,000

Transactions during 2002 and other information related to stockholders' equity accounts were as follows:
(1) On January 10, 2002, Norway issued at $110 per share 100,000 shares of $100 pare value, 8% cumulative preferred stock.
(2) On February 8, 2002, Norway reacquired 10,000 shares of its common stock for $16 per share.
(3) On June 8, 2002, Norway declared a cash dividend of $1 per share on the common stock outstanding, payable on July 10, 2002, to stockholders of record on July 1, 2002.
(4) On December 15, 2002, Norway declared the yearly cash dividend on preferred stock, payable January 10, 2003, to stockholders of record on December 15, 2002.
(5) Net income for the year was $3,600,000.
(6) It was discovered that depreciation expense has been overstated in 2001 by $100,000.

Instructions:
(a) Prepare a retained earnings statement for the year ended December 31, 2002.
(b) Prepare the stockholders' equity section of Norway's balance sheet at December 31, 2002.

CHAPTER 13

INVESTMENTS

CHAPTER OUTLINE

CLUES, HINTS, AND TIPS

Goal seek

Goal seek is one of the tools within Excel that will provide you the answer. With Goal seek you click into a cell containing a formula then follow the path Tools>Goal Seek and respond to the dialog box. The worksheet in the screen print is in the chapter 13 data file, chptr13 with the title of Goal Seek. The path, Tools>Goal Seek, is shown on the screen print. The pop-up dialog box requires that you identify a cell with a formula in it, for the example that cell is C4. Then enter the number you want the formula to end up at, 20 as shown in the screen print. Then tell Goal Seek what cell you want the value inserted into to create the answer of 20. This cell must be referenced in the formula cell, C4. For the example cell C3 was chosen. When OK is clicked with the mouse or the enter key is struck, Excel will produce a pop-up text box stating that it found a solution to get the value of 20 and that that value is 17 and it asks if this is acceptable. Since it is, click on the OK and Excel will modify the value in cell C3 to 17 and close out. If the answer is unacceptable hit Cancel and the value will be left at 3. If Excel cannot compute the value it will error out and tell you it cannot find a solution. This is usually because cell identified in the By changing cell window is not within the formula contained within the Set Cell window.

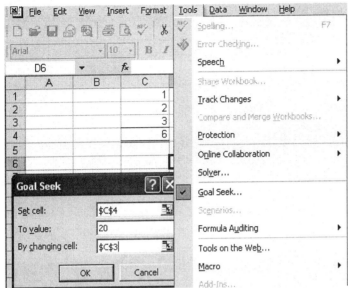

If statements

As shown and utilized through the templates and Clues, Hints, and Tips, the If statement is a very powerful and easy to use logic tool. The If statement works on the principle of comparing term one with term two and if the terms make the condition true, it replies with the first field after the comparison, if it is false, it replies with the second. The first or second field can be another if statement, formula, or text. The formula format is =IF(2=2,4,0). In this simple if statement if 2 equals 2 the formula will put 4 in the cell, if 2 does not equal 2 the formula will put 0 in the cell. Since 2 does equal 2 the response will be 4. However the statement =IF(2=Two,4,0) will result in an error presentation since text strings inside formulas must be contained within quotation marks such as =IF(2="Two",4,0). If this statement is entered into Excel on the If Statements tab, the response will be 0 as the number 2 is not equal to a text string of the letters T, w, and o. As stated earlier, Excel does not read English, but it can compare text strings through spell check, F7.

Excel will compare text strings and provide responses. For example the statement =IF("Two"="Two",4,0) will return the value 4 not because it is the sum but because it is the first field or the "True" term following a true statement. There is a detail of Excel that needs to be appreciated in all of the comparative statements. If the value of 123.456 is entered into a cell with formatting to display two decimal places the entered value will display as 123.45 but Excel will remember and respond as if it is 123.456. If this value is compared to a displayed value of 123.45 which is in a cell formatted to display two decimal places but the value is actually 123.4567, the values appear to be equal, as presented in the formatted cells but they are not. Try it on the If Statement tab of the chapter data file. When Excel compares values and one value is formatted to currency and the other formatted to general, for example, Excel will ignore the formatting and compare the values.

The following is a table containing most of the comparison operators available to the if statement:

= (equal sign) if the first comparative term is equal to the second comparative term, the first field or the true field will be returned, if the comparison is false, the second field or the false field will be returned. Your question is "Is it true that the first comparative term is equal to the second comparative term?" The answer is True or False and the caused response is the first field or the true field or the second field, the false field.

Hint – Try to think of questions that are answered True/False with If statements.

<> (not equal to sign) (The order of the operators is important!) If the first comparative term is **_NOT_** equal to the second comparative term, the first field or the true field will be returned, if the comparison is false, the second field or the false field will be returned. Your question is "Is it true that the first comparative term is **_NOT_** equal to the second comparative term?" The answer is True or False and the caused response is the first field or the true field or the second field, the false field.

> (greater than sign) If the first comparative term is greater than the second comparative term, the first field or the true field will be returned, if the comparison is false, the second field or the false field will be returned. Your question is "Is it true that the first comparative term is greater than the second

comparative term?" The answer is True or False and the caused response is the first field or the true field or the second field, the false field.

< (less than sign) If the first comparative term is less than the second comparative term, the first field or the true field will be returned, if the comparison is false, the second field or the false field will be returned. Your question is "Is it true that the first comparative term is less than the second comparative term?" The answer is True or False and the caused response is the first field or the true field or the second field, the false field.

>= (greater than or equal to sign) (The order of the operators is important!) If the first comparative term is greater than or equal to the second comparative term, the first field or the true field will be returned, if the comparison is false, the second field or the false field will be returned. Your question is "Is it true that the first comparative term is greater than or equal to the second comparative term?" The answer is True or False and the caused response is the first field or the true field or the second field, the false field.

<= (less than or equal to sign) (The order of the operators is important!) If the first comparative term is less than the second comparative term, the first field or the true field will be returned, if the comparison is false, the second field or the false field will be returned. Your question is "Is it true that the first comparative term is less than or equal to the second comparative term?" The answer is True or False and the caused response is the first field or the true field or the second field, the false field.

If statements can be imbedded in other formulas and can be embedded within themselves. The maximum is seven layers deep. However, with the ability of Excel to run an if statement on the results of an if statement, the seven layer depth restriction is of little concern.

Subtotal

Subtotal is a tool that requires more show than text to explain. Subtotal requires that the worksheet be sorted by the basic order for the subtotaling operation. In a worksheet such as the one on the Subtotal tab of the chapter 13 data file built for this purpose the sort should by Item then by State then by Quantity.

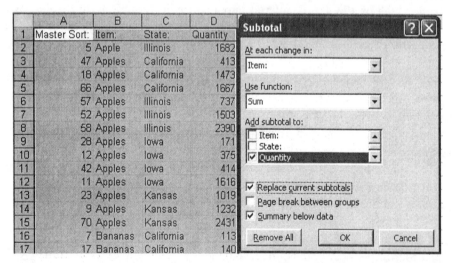

Since row 1 is a frozen pane and contains the titles Excel should present these as sort criteria. Refer the Sort article earlier in the booklet if necessary. Next, select the entire worksheet through the select all button or the Ctrl-A key strokes. If the data is only contained on a small part of a larger worksheet you can highlight only the area of interest.

Once the worksheet is selected follow the path Data>Subtotal and a pop-up menu will appear. This menu is shown here. The first window, "At each change in" controls the major events of this function. Select Items from the drop down menu. This will cause the subtotal function to create a new subtotal bracket for each change in the column titled Item. This is why the sort process was essential prior to subtotaling. In the Use Function window insure it reads "Sum". Other options are available and can be used at another time. In the Add subtotal to window check the Quantity option. This will cause the subtotal function to add the quantities and give us subtotals for each break in Items. Insure that Replace existing subtotals is checked and that summary data below is checked. If page break between groups is selected you may consume excessive paper when printing but for distribution of inventory data, this is a nice feature. Click OK and Excel will perform the subtotal.

The result is a worksheet that summarizes the inventory as you had sorted it. You now know the number of apples and bananas and whatever else. By scrolling down to the bottom of the worksheet you will see a summary of the data giving you a grand total – the result of the summary at the bottom option.

This result can be a final but we will use it as an intermediate. Select the entire sheet and follow the path Data>Subtotal again. This time select State in the At each change in window. Then remove the check mark from replace existing subtotals in the lower portion of the dialog box and click OK. Now you have a worksheet that is sorted and displayed by item, state, and quantity and subtotaled to present the amount of each item in each state with subtotals showing the amount of apples, bananas and so forth. On the left side of the window a new set of scroll bars appeared. By clicking on the 1, 2, 3, or 4 various degrees of detail will be hidden by Excel. Clicking them again makes them reappear – another toggle. With the new scroll bars you can make various detail lines disappear from the display without hiding all of the items at that level. As shown, there can be multiple layers of subtotals to suit your needs.

To remove subtotal from the worksheet follow the path Data>Subtotal again to the pop-up dialog box. This time select the Remove all option and click OK. Excel removes the subtotal features.

The worksheet has been setup with a master sort column, addressed earlier, so that randomness can be reintroduced after the exercise is run by sorting on the master sort column.

Vlookup

Vlookup is another powerful presentation tool of Excel that takes more show than text to explain. There is a tab set up in the chapter 13 data file titled Vlookup for this explanation. The formula is located under the Lookup and Reference category and looks like this: =VLOOKUP(F2,$A$1:$D$71,2,FALSE). The value F2 is the reference to the value Vlookup is seeking in the table defined by the cells A1 through D71. Excel does not put absolute references into the formula so these were inserted so the formula could be dragged down the Vlookup tab worksheet. The 2 is telling Excel to return the value found in the second column of the table. This is not column B except by coincidence. Excel counts columns from the left most column of the table towards the right. If you look at the formulas in columns G, H, and I of row 2 you will see that each returns a different column number. The false statement at the end of the formula is telling Excel if you do not find the EXACT value return nothing – Excel will respond with a #N/A# display. If the statement is left out or True and Excel does not find an exact match Excel will return the value immediately before exceeding the search value.

On the Vlookup tab there is a matrix from cell F2 to F20 with numbers placed in them. Written into the matrix defined by G2 through I20 is a grouping of Vlookup formulas looking at this feeder matrix. Replacing a number in column F will cause the Vlookup formulas in columns G through I to scan the first column and first column only of the table defined in the formula as A1 through D71 for that number. If the function finds an exact match as controlled by the true statement Excel will return the values of the second column of the table in column G, the value found in the third column in column H, and the value found in the fourth column in column I.

Tip - If the same value is placed in column F more than once Vlookup and Excel do not care. They will return the requested value as often as requested. Therefore, caution should be utilized if Vlookup is being to return value or quantity.

Vlookup is structured for data in a vertical format. If your data is in a horizontal format utilize Hlookup.

EXERCISES

Exercise E13-5 (File 13e-5) Journalize entries under the cost and equity methods

Presented below are two independent situations:

(a) Roscoe Cosmetics acquired 10% of the 200,000 shares of common stock of Ling Fashinon at a total cost of $13 per share on March 18, 2002. On June 30, Ling declared and paid a $75,000 dividend. On December 31, Ling reported net income of $122,000 for the year. At December 31, the market price of Ling Fashion was $14 per share. The stock is classified as available-for-sale.

(b) Juan, Inc., obtained significant influence over Orlando Corporation by buying 30% of Orlando's 30,000 outstanding shares of common stock at a total cost of $9 per share on January 1, 2002. On June 15, Orlando declared and paid a cash dividend of $35,000. On December 31, Orlando reported a net income of $80,000 for the year.

Instructions:
Prepare all the necessary journal entries for 2002 for (a) Roscoe Cosmetics and (b) Juan, Inc.

Exercise E13-6 (File 13e-6) Prepare adjusting entry to record fair value, and indicate statement presentation

At December 31, 2002, the trading securities for Yanu, Inc. are as follows:

Security	Cost	Fair value
A	$17,500	$16,000
B	12,500	14,000
C	23,000	19,000
	$53,000	$49,000

Instructions:
(a) Prepare the adjusting entry at December 31, 2002, to report the securities at fair value.
(b) Show the balance sheet and income statement presentation at December 31, 2002, after adjustment to fair value.

PROBLEMS

Problem P13-2A (File 13p-2a) Journalize investment transactions, prepare adjusting entry, and show statement presentation

In January 2002, the management of Harris Company concludes that it has sufficient cash to permit some short-term investments in debt and stock securities. During the year, the following transactions occurred:

Feb 1   Purchased 400 shares of Alpha common stock for $21,800, plus brokerage fees of $600.

Mar 1   Purchased 800 shares of Omega common stock for $20,000, plus brokerage fees of $400.

Apr 1   Purchased 40 $1,000, 12% Pep bonds for $40,000, plus $1,000 brokerage fees. Interest is payable semiannually on April 1 and October 1.

July 1   Received a cash dividend of $0.60 per share on Alpha common stock.

Aug 1   Sold 200 shares of Alpha common stock at $58 per share less brokerage fees of $200.

Sep 1   Received a $1 per share cash dividend on the Omega common stock.

Oct 1   Received the semiannual interest on the Pep bonds.

Oct 1   Sold the Pep bonds for $41,000 less $1,000 brokerage fees.

At December 31, the fair value of the Alpha common stock was $55 per share. The fair value of the Omega common stock was $23 per share.

Instructions:

(a) Journalize the transactions and post to the accounts Debt investments and Stock investments. (Use the T-account format.)

(b) Prepare the adjusting entry at December 31, 2002, to report the investment securities at fair value. All securities are considered to be trading securities.

(c) Show the balance sheet presentation of investment securities at December 31, 2002.

(d) Identify the income statement accounts and give the statement classification of each account.

Problem P13-3A (File 13p-3a) Journalize transactions and adjusting entry for stock investments

On December 31, 2002 Melanie Associates owned the following securities, held as a long-term investment. The securities are not held for influence or control of the investee.

Common stock	Shares	Cost
Carson Co.	6,000	$90,000
Pirie Co	5,000	45,000
Scott Co.	1,500	30,000

On this date, the total fair value of the securities was equal to its cost. In 2003, the following transactions occurred:

Jul 1   Received $1 per share semiannual cash dividend on Pirie Co. common stock.

Aug 1   Received $0.50 per share cash dividend on Carson Co. common stock.

Sep 1   Sold 1,000 shares of Pirie Co. common stock for cash at $8 per share, less brokerage fees of $200.

Oct 1   Sold 800 shares of Carson Co. common stock for cash at $17 per share, less brokerage fees of $500.

Nov 1   Received $1 per share cash dividend on Scott Co. common stock.

Dec 15   Received $0.50 per share cash dividend on Carson Co. common stock.

Dec 31   Received $1 per share semiannual cash dividend on Pirie Co. common stock.

At December 31, the fair values per share of the common stocks were:

Common stock	Value per share
Carson Co.	$16
Pirie Co	$8
Scott Co.	$18

Instructions:

(a) Journalize the 2003 transactions and post to the account Stock investments. (Use the T-account format.)

(b) Prepare the adjusting entry at December 31, 2003, to show the securities at fair value. The stock should be classified as available-for-sale securities.

(c) Show the balance sheet presentation of the investments at December 31, 2003. At this date, Melanie Associates has common stock $1,500,000 and retained earnings of $1,000,000.

Problem P13-6A (File 13p-6a) Prepare balance sheet

The following data, presented in alphabetical order, are taken from the records of Scheer Corporation:

Accounts payable	$250,000
Accounts receivable	140,000
Accumulated depreciation-Building	180,000
Accumulated depreciation-Equipment	52,000
Allowance for doubtful accounts	6,000
Bonds payable (10%, due 2013)	500,000
Bond sinking fund	150,000
Buildings	950,000
Cash	72,000
Common stock (410 par value, 500,000 shares authorized, 150,000 shares issued)	1,500,000
Dividends payable	80,000
Equipment	275,000
Goodwill	200,000
Income taxes payable	120,000
Investments in Lotto common stock (10% ownership), at cost	278,000
Investments in Portico common stock (30% ownership), at equity	230,000
Land	500,000
Market adjustment-available-for-sale securities (Dr.)	8,000
Merchandise inventory	170,000
Notes payable (due 2003)	70,000
Paid-in capital in excess of par value	200,000
Premium on bonds payable	40,000
Prepaid insurance	16,000
Retained earnings	163,000
Short-term stock investment, at fair value (and cost)	180,000
Unrealized gain-available-for-sale securities	8,000

The investment in Lotto common stock is considered to be a long-term available-for-sale security.

Instructions:

Prepare a balance sheet at December 31, 2002.

Problem P13-2B (File 13p-2b) Journalize investment transactions, prepare adjusting entry, and show statement presentation

In January 2002, the management of Wolfe Company concludes that it as sufficient cash to purchase some short-term investments in debt and stock securities. During the year, the following transactions occurred:

Feb 1   Purchased 800 shares of LRT common stock for $32,000, plus brokerage fees of $800.

Mar 1   Purchased 500 shares of IMA common stock for $15,000, plus brokerage fees of $300.

Apr 1   Purchased 40 $1,000, 12% CAL bonds for $40,000, plus $1,200 brokerage fees. Interest is payable semiannually on April 1 and October 1.

July 1   Received a cash dividend of $0.60 per share on LRT common stock.

Aug 1   Sold 300 shares of LRT common stock at $42 per share, less brokerage fees of $350.

Sep 1   Received a $1 per share cash dividend on the IMA common stock.

Oct 1   Received the semiannual interest on the CAL bonds.

Oct 1   Sold the CAL bonds for $44,000 less $1,000 brokerage fees.

At December 31, the fair value of the LRT common stock was $39 per share. The fair value of the IMA common stock was $30 per share.

Instructions:

(a) Journalize the transactions and post to the accounts Debt investments and Stock investments. (Use the T-account format.)

(b) Prepare the adjusting entry at December 31, 2002, to report the investment securities at fair value. All securities are considered to be trading securities.

(c) Show the balance sheet presentation of investment securities at December 31, 2002.

(d) Identify the income statement accounts and give the statement classification of each account.

Problem P13-5B (File 13p-5b) Journalize stock transactions and show statement presentation

The following are in Barry Bonds Company's portfolio of long-term available-for-sale securities at December 31, 2002:

Company	Type	Nbr of shares	Cost
McGwire Corporation	Common	500	$26,000
B. Ruth Corporation	Common	700	$42,000
H. Aaron Corporation	Preferred	400	$16,800

On December 31, the total cost of the portfolio equaled total fair value. Barry Bonds Company had the following transactions related to the securities during 2003:

Jan 7   Sold 500 shares of McGwire Corporation common stock at $56 per share less brokerage fees of $700.

Jan 10   Purchased 200 shares, $70 par value, common stock of Mantle Corporation at $78 per share, plus brokerage fees of $240.

Jan 26   Received a cash dividend of $1.15 per share on B. Ruth Corporation common stock.

Feb 2   Received a cash dividend of $0.40 per share on H. Aaron Corporation preferred stock.

Feb 10 Sold all 400 shares of H. Aaron Corporation preferred stock at $35 per share less brokerage fees of $180.

July 1 Received a cash dividend of $1.00 per share on B. Ruth Corporation common stock.

Sep 1   Purchased an additional 400 shares of the $70 par value, common stock of Mantle Corporation at $75 per share, plus brokerage fees of $400.

Dec 15 Received a cash dividend of $1.50 per share on Mantle Corporation common stock.

At December 31, 2003, the fair values of the securities were:

B. Ruth Corporation common stock	$63 per share
Mantle Corporation common stock	$72 per share

Barry Bonds Company uses separate account titles for each investment, such as Investment in B. Ruth Corporation common stock.

Instructions:

(a) Prepare journal entries to record the transactions.

(b) Post to the investment account. (Use the T-account format.)

(c) Prepare the adjusting entry at December 31, 2003, to report the portfolio at fair value.

(d) Show the balance sheet presentation at December 31, 2003.

CHAPTER 14

THE STATEMENT OF CASH FLOWS

CHAPTER OUTLINE

CLUES, HINTS, AND TIPS

Charting

Excel will assist you in making charts through the Chart Wizard. This wizard is accessed through the charting icon on the task bar shown here. There are operational examples of charts on the Charting tab of the chapter 14 data file, chptr14. One of the most important concerns in charting is picking an appropriate chart type for your data. In the examples in the data file the information supplied is Sales items, Sales costs per sales item, and Sales revenues per sale item. This information is charted as examples in several ways. The use of the two charts titled Sales costs and Sales revenues are both pie charts, appropriate for the conveyance of the information, clear, and somewhat attractive. However, the goal is to show the relationship between costs and sales of the individual item and that relationship to the other sales items. With the information contained on the two pie charts, this relationship must be made in the mind of the reader. By utilizing the Bar chart this relationship is clear and distinct in a single chart. To the right of these charts are an Area chart and a Surface chart. The area chart infers that there is a flow from a span of time or events that is not correct even though, at points on the chart, it does convey the visual relationship between cost and sales revenues for an item and the relationships between products. In the surface chart the information is totally unclear as to purpose, value, and intent. For this example data, the Bar chart is probably the best visual presentation. To obtain the best guidance as to which chart to use to convey what information, scan your text books as well as professional magazines conveying the same type of information and look at the chart or graph styles used by the professional.

The quickest way to build a chart within Excel is to highlight the data range before selecting the Chart Wizard. For the data file, this is from cell A1 through C6. You can use the data on the Working Chart Area tab of the data file if you desire for this demonstration. The incorporation of the totals line may add an additional, unwanted, field that would have to be removed later. Now click on the Chart Wizard icon. The Chart Wizard will walk you through the process first by selecting a chart type. Excel has many chart types and by utilizing the "Press and hold to view sample" button at the bottom of the Wizard box you will see your data in the chart mode selected – one reason why your data was highlighted before selecting the Chart Wizard icon. Since charts are easily made, edited and removed, try any chart you desire – except a valid type for the data. A correction mode will be shown later. With the (incorrect) chart type picked, click on the Next button and the Chart Wizard will ask you to confirm the data range and series. Check both tabs. If satisfied, click on the Next button, if not; modify the data as desired or back up to the previous screen utilizing the Back button. The data portrayed in the chart does not affect the source data. When the Next button is clicked, the Chart Wizard will ask for Chart titles, axis titles and other items for the chart. Some of these items may not be available because of the chart type selected, some may be filled in with information the Chart Wizard "learned" from the data. Enter what you desire and the Wizard will show you a working model of your chart as you build it. Under the Data Table tab, if presented, you can select an option to show the source data with the chart. A very nice feature for some data presentations. When satisfied, click the Next button and ensure that the chart will be placed on the current sheet, the default selection by the Wizard, click the Finish button. The Wizard will finish your chart.

If your chart does not seem large enough – not all of the data is visible, you can drag the chart away from the border of the worksheet. You can also change its size by clicking on the chart and getting "Frame ears" or "handles" to appear on the exterior borders of the chart, then grab one of these with the mouse and drag the chart into a larger (or smaller) size. Be aware that the chart consists of many objects and clicking into the chart and getting "Frame ears" or "handles" inside the exterior frame means you have grabbed an object in the chart, not the overall chart.

Your chart is finished but since you selected an inappropriate chart presentation for your data, your chart does not clearly portray the information. No problem. Like many things in Excel, your chart is a dynamic, live, object. Right click into the chart and select Chart Type from the pop-up menu. You are back into the Chart Wizard and can select a more appropriate chart type and preview it again if desired. By right clicking the chart you can gain access to many of the chart functions, features and capabilities. This includes being able to format fonts. You can also add, remove, and reposition labels. Try clicking on a label, once "Frame ears" or "handles" appear, strike the delete key and the label goes away.

The chart can be copied and pasted elsewhere. The chart is "live" – if the source data changes, the chart changes.

Go to

With Excel worksheets as large as they are you frequently traverse to various areas via the scroll bars, the tab key, the enter key or the arrow keys. Excel has a "Go to" function accessed by the key strokes Ctrl-G or through the path Edit>Go to. The pop-up dialog box asks where to? And you can enter a cell address such as A4 and click OK. And you are there. If you have named ranges, as exists on the Working Chart Area tab, when you invoke the Go to command, you will be presented with those areas in the dialog box for quick and easy selection. Another reason to name a cell or a range of cells within Excel.

Key strokes & Shortcuts

There are many key strokes that work in a standard Windows format regardless of the program. Some are unique to the program. Here are some simple and useful key strokes for Excel:

The key strokes of Ctrl-Home (key strokes not type in entry) will take you to cell A1 unless the defaults are changed.

The key stroke of Home will take you to column A of the row with the currently active cell.

Page up will change the screen displayed up one "pane" of cells. If the top row is row 128, page up will make the bottom row on the new screen 127. If there is not enough rows available because of the upper or lower limit of Excel, nothing will happen.

Page down will change the screen displayed down one "pane" of cells. If the bottom row is row 128, page down will make the top row on the new screen 129. If there is not enough rows available because of the upper or lower limit of Excel, nothing will happen.

Arrow keys will move you one cell up, right, down, or left for each striking, if held, they will scroll you in the selected direction. If you have edited the data within a cell, the use of the arrow keys will not let you leave the cell. Tab or enter must be struck or you must click into another cell with the mouse.

Ctrl-A selects all cells on the worksheet.

Ctrl-B toggles the selected cell or range of cells into and out of bold text mode.

Ctrl-C copies the selected cell or range of cells.

Ctrl-D is fill down.

Ctrl-F brings up the find and find and replace dialog box.

Ctrl-G brings up the go to dialog box.

Ctrl- H brings up the find and find and replace dialog box.

Ctrl-I toggles the selected cell or range of cells into and out of italics text mode.

Ctrl-K brings up the hyper link dialog box.

Ctrl-N opens a new worksheet.

Ctrl-O brings up the Open worksheet dialog box.

Ctrl-P brings up the print dialog box.

Ctrl-R is fill right

Ctrl-S saves the file if it has been saved before, it brings up the save dialog box if this is the first save.

Ctrl-Y is repeat options.

Ctrl-X is cut the cell or range of cells.

Ctrl-Z is undo clear

Ctrl-` - the accent character on usually to the left of the 1/! Key brings up the audit tool bar.

Ctrl-1 (The number one) is format cell or cells.

F1 (The number 1) brings up the Help screen.

F7 starts spell-check

Macros

Macros are small programs that you can build out of key stroke modeling – you record them by doing what you normally do for later, repetative use. To record a macro ensure you know the key strokes and commands you desire to utilize in the macro. If you record an error in a macro you will have to edit the macro or rerecord it. Place your curser into cell A10 of the Macro tab in the data file and make that cell the active cell. You will build a simple macro for demonstration purposes that formats the cell to bold, italics, and underline a cell in a single event. Bring up the macro dialog box by following the path Tools>Macro>Record New Macro. You will be asked for the name of the new macro and where you would like it stored. The name should not have spaces or special characters in it. Excel will tell you if the title is unacceptable. The demonstration macro was named BoldItalicsUnderline so try BIU for your macro. In the Store Macro In window select This Workbook. This will contain the macro to the data file and this workbook. The dialog box asks if you want to assign a control key to the macro – enter the character "m" as a lower case letter without striking any other key. Click on the OK and Excel will commence record the macro.

Tip – To see if a control key is assigned a function in Excel, click into Excel and try the key sequence. If Excel gives you a dull thud response, the key command was not recognized or it is unavailable at the moment.

Once Excel starts recording the macro, everything you do will be recorded. Click into cell A2 then click the Bold icon, the Italics icon, and the Underline icon on the task bar. Then click on the stop recording button on the macro dialog box the appeared on the screen. This is a square button. When you click the stop recording button your macro is stored and available for use.

Now click into cell A3 and run the macro through the key strokes Ctrl-m or through the path Tools>Macro>Macros and click on the BIU select and click run. The error with the macro is that it goes to cell A2 and puts bold, italics, and underline on cell A2. This is because the first thing you told the macro to do was go to cell A2. Now we will edit the macro to preclude it from moving to cell A2 each time. Follow the path Tools>Macro>Macros and select BIU then select Edit from the button choices. The macro tools and the Microsoft Visual Basic window will open and you will see the macro command strings. One of the command strings reads "Range("A2").Select". Highlight and delete this one line then close the window. You have now edited (corrected) the macro. Click into cell A3 and invoke the macro with the key strokes Ctrl-m and cell A3 should become bold, italics, and underlined.

Macros are powerful tools. They can be absolutes – go to cell A2 – as we originally recorded BIU. Or they can be focused on the target cell or the active cell. Macros will format worksheets, enter data, run spell checks and almost any other repetitive task you have.

Clear and Cut

To Excel clear and cut are two different commands. The clear command under the path Edit>Clear or on the pop-up menu you are presented with when you right click a cell or range of cells deletes the information from the cell or range of cells without posting it to the clipboard for later use. If you want to recover the information it may be available through the undo command.

The Cut command is available through the path Edit>Cut, on the pop-up menu you are presented with when you right click a cell or range of cells, or by using the Scissors icon on the tool bar when a cell or range of cells is active or highlighted. The item or items in the cut cell or cells is not moved until you select a target cell or range of cells and paste the cut cells in. Cut is a one time pasting event. If you want to paste the cell or range of cells in several locations, cut is not the tool, use copy. Cut allows you to place the data once. Once pasted, the new area is currently highlighted so you can copy it without reselecting it. Formulas moved by cut retain their original references, formulas copied and pasted are moved relationally.

EXERCISES

Exercise E14-5 (File 14e-5) Prepare a statement of cash flows-Indirect method

Comparative balance sheets for Eddie Murphy Company are presented below:

EDDIE MURPHY COMPANY
Comparative Balance Sheet
December 31

Assets	2002	2001
Cash	$63,000	$22,000
Accounts receivable	85,000	76,000
Inventories	180,000	189,000
Land	75,000	100,000
Equipment	260,000	200,000
Accumulated depreciation	(66,000)	(42,000)
Total	$597,000	$545,000
Liabilities and Stockholders' equity		
Accounts payable	34,000	47,000
Bonds payable	150,000	200,000
Common stock ($1 par)	214,000	164,000
Retained earnings	199,000	134,000
Total	$597,000	$545,000

Additional information:
   (1) Net income for 2002 was $125,000.
   (2) Cash dividends of $60,000 were declared and paid.
   (3) Bonds payable amounting to $50,000 were redeemed for cash $50,000.
   (4) Common stock was issued for $50,000 cash.
   (5) Depreciation expense was $24,000.
   (6) Sales for the year were $978,000.

Instructions:
(a) Prepare a statement of cash flows for 2002 using the indirect method.
(b) Compute the following cash-basis ratios:
   (1) Current cash debt coverage ratio.
   (2) Cash return on sales ratio.
   (3) Cash debt coverage ratio.

Exercise E14-9 (File 14e-9) Compute cash flow from operating activities-Direct method

The 2002 accounting records of Winona Ryder Co. reveals the following transactions and events:

Payment of interest	$6,000	Payment of salaries and wages	$65,000
Cash sales	38,000	Depreciation expense	18,000
Receipt of dividend revenue	14,000	Proceeds from sale of aircraft	812,000
Payment of income taxes	15,000	Purchase of equip for cash	22,000
Net income	38,000	Loss on sale of aircraft	3,000
Payment of A/P for merchandise	90,000	Payment of dividends	14,000
Payment for land	74,000	Payment of operating expense	20,000
Collection of accounts receivable	180,000		

Instructions:
Prepare the cash flows from operating activities section of the statement of cash flows using the direct method. (Not all of the above items will be used.)

PROBLEMS

Problem P14-7A (File 14p-7a) Prepare a statement of cash flows-Indirect method

Condensed financial data of Tom Cruise Company appear below:

TOM CRUISE COMPANY
Comparative Balance Sheets
December 31

Assets	2002	2001
Cash	$92,700	$47,250
Accounts receivable	90,800	57,000
Inventories	121,900	102,650
Investments	84,500	87,000
Plant assets	250,000	205,000
Accumulated depreciation	(49,500)	(40,000)
Total	$590,400	$458,900
Liabilities and Stockholders' equity		
Accounts payable	$57,700	$48,280
Accrued expenses payable	12,100	18,830
Bonds payable	100,000	70,000
Common stock	250,000	200,000
Retained earnings	170,600	121,790
Total	$590,400	$458,900

TOM CRUISE COMPANY
Income Statement Data
For the Year Ended December 31, 2002

Sales		$297,500
Gain on sale of plant assets		8,750
		306,250
Less:		
Cost of goods sold	$99,460	
Operating expenses (excluding depreciation exp)	14,670	
Depreciation expense	49,700	
Income taxes	7,270	
Interest expense	2,940	174,040
Net income		$132,210

Additional information:
(1) New plant assets costing $92,000 were purchased for cash during the year.
(2) Investments were sold at cost.
(3) Plant assets costing $47,000 were sold for $15,500, resulting in a gain of $8,750.
(4) A cash dividend of $83,400 was declared and paid during the year.

Instructions:
Prepare a statement of cash flows using the indirect method.

Problem P14-8A (File 14p-8a) Prepare a statement of cash flows-Direct method

Data for Tom Cruise Company are presented in P14-7A. Further analysis reveals that accounts payable pertains to merchandise creditors.

Instructions:
Prepare a statement of cash flows for Tom Cruise Company using the direct method.

Problem P14-3B (File 14p-3b) Prepare the operating activities section-Direct method

George Clooney Company's income statement for the year ended December 31, 2002, contained the following condensed information:

Revenue from fees		$900,000
Operating expenses (excluding depreciation)	$624,000	
Depreciation expense	60,000	
Loss on sale of equipment	26,000	710,000
Income before income taxes		190,000
Income tax expense		40,000
Net income		$150,000

Clooney's balance sheet contained the following comparative data at December 31:

	2002	2001
Accounts receivable	$47,000	$57,000
Accounts payable	41,000	36,000
Income taxes payable	4,000	9,000

(Accounts payable pertains to operating expenses.)

Instructions:
Prepare the operating activities section of the statement of cash flows for George Clooney Company using the direct method.

Problem P14-4B (File 14p-4b) Prepare the operating activities section-Indirect method

Data for George Clooney Company is presented in P14-3B.

Instructions:
Prepare the operating activities section of the statement of cash flows for George Clooney Company using the indirect method.

CHAPTER 15

FINANCIAL STATEMENT ANALYSIS

CLUES, HINTS, AND TIPS

Hiding columns and rows

Excel will allow you to hide a column, columns, row or rows. The methodology is to highlight the column, columns, row or rows. For each operation these must be adjacent. Then follow the path Edit>Hide from the task bar or right click the highlighted area and select Hide from the pop-up menu. Once the cell or cells are hidden you will see that the column identifiers and row numbers do not appear to follow the usual sequence. As shown on the chapter 15 data file, chptr15, Hidden tab you can see that columns B, D, and F as well as rows such as 5 and 6 are hidden. If you examine the border lines between the column identifiers and the row identifiers you will see a slight difference in their presentation if there are hidden columns or rows there. These cells remain active in all formula and will still be active for functions like Go to, Find, and Find and replace. This technique is excellent for extended calculations that are not desired in the presentation. However, copy and paste commands are active on these cells and caution needs to be exercised when a cell or cell is hidden.

    To unhide a cell or cells you have several options. Highlight the predecessor and successor columns or rows that border the hidden columns or rows and follow the path Edit>Unhide from the menu bar or right click the highlighted area and select Unhide from the pop-up menu. There is also hide and unhide options through Format>Column or Format>Row from the menu bar.

    In the chapter data file there are numerous areas for you to hide and unhide.

Column and row size

The size of the columns and rows can be adjusted within Excel in several manners. The first is to "grab" the right border of a column or the bottom border of a row with the mouse and the left mouse button depressed when it becomes a double headed arrow and drag it to the size you desire. If you highlight more than one column or row at a time, whether adjacent or not, they will all resize to the same value at the same time. Remember that you can select or highlight nonadjacent areas by holding the control key down while clicking the columns or rows with the mouse.

An alternative is to "Autosize" the column or row by placing your cursor over the right border of a column or the bottom border of a row and double clicking it with the mouse. This increases the column or row's size quickly to the largest item in the column or row. ***DO NOT DO THIS ON THE TEMPLATES.*** Many of the templates have long text strings in them with center justification and this will cause rapid growth of the worksheet. Another method of sizing a column or row is to highlight the column or row and follow the path Format>Column or Format>Row, as appropriate, and select what action you want. With the Width or Height option you will be asked to manually enter a value. For a column the default width is approximately the width of 0123456789 in default font. For a row the default height is 12.75. If you resize a column or row to a width wider than the screen you can resize it through the path Format>Column or Format>Row and select Width or Height and set to a value of approximately 10 for the column width or 12.75 for the row to return it to near default value.

If you have a column or row highlighted you will also find width and height setting options on the pop-up menu if you right click the highlighted column or row.

Conditional formatting

Excel will accept several levels of formatting for a cell under the path of Format>Conditional Format. On the chapter 15 data file Conditional Formatting tab there is an example in cell A1. If the value is less then 1 the cell appears normal, if the cell contains a value between one and ten, the formatting is horrible, if the value is greater than 10 the formatting gets worse. While this was done for effect, if you were inputting mark-ups for retail and wanted no percentage less than 50% nor more than 150%, you could format the cell to go red if the percentage is not within this range as cell A3 is formatted to.

By examining the drop-down menu selection choices of the operator, defaulted to "between" you will see that you have a wide range of operators to work with. You can impose up to three levels of conditional formatting on a cell by clicking on the Add button at the bottom of the dialog box. If you have imposed conditional formatting on a cell you can remove one or more levels of formatting by following the path Format>Conditional Format while the target cell is selected and clicking delete.

Pivot tables

A pivot table is the presentation of data with multiple classifications such as district, salesman, and quantity of various items sold. The chapter 15 data file, chptr15, contains a data matrix for the construction of a pivot table. One of the requirements of a pivot table is that you must have two layers of classification on the left side, at least one layer of classification on the top, and data at the intersections of the classifications. This data need not be presorted or arranged, the Pivot Table Wizard will handle that for you. For the example column A is region – North, South, East, or West, column B contains the salesman's name, row 1 contains the items sold, and the data for each region is contained in the matrix defined by the cells C2 through I32.

As with the Chart Wizard, it is handier to highlight the information before you start the Pivot Table Wizard. So, highlight the range from A1 through I32. This will incorporate labels, titles, and data. Then follow the path Tools>Pivot Table and Pivot Table Chart Reports…. The Wizard's dialog box will appear asking you what you would like to accomplish and where is the data. Ensure that you are using Excel data in the upper selection and that a Pivot Table is selected in the lower portion of the dialog box, then click nest. The Pivot Table Wizard should present you with a confirmation that you are using the range A1 through I32 for the data, confirm this and click next. The next dialog box asks "Where do you want the table to appear?", select on a new worksheet and click Finish. Excel presents you with a blank table that is used to build the table itself. From the Pivot table field list drag the "Region" item to the top of the pivot table where it says "Drop column fields here", then drag the "Salesman" item to the area where it says "Drop row fields here", then drag each of the sales items into the center grid where it says "Drop data items here". As you drop your items on the table Excel will start working. As you drop each item, the item will change go **bold** print in the list to indicate that it has been used.

The resulting table will show you who is selling what items where as well as the totals sold for the item and the totals sold in each region. Through the use of the filters, activated through the drop down arrows on the titles, you can control what is displayed. Pivot tables are memory intensive events for the computer. If you are limited as to the number for fields or it takes more than a couple of seconds to generate this table that can be expected.

EXERCISES

Exercise E15-4 (File 15e-4) Prepare horizontal and vertical analysis

The comparative income statements of Sondgeroth Corporation are shown below:

SONDGEROTH CORPORATION
Comparative Income Statements
For the Years Ended December 31

	2003	2002
Net sales	$600,000	$500,000
Cost of goods sold	450,000	420,000
Gross profit	150,000	80,000
Operating expenses	57,200	44,000
Net income	$92,800	$36,000

Instructions:
(a) Prepare a horizontal analysis of the income statement data for Sondgeroth Corporation using 2002 as a base. (Show the amounts of increase or decrease.)
(b) Prepare a vertical analysis of the income statement data for Sondgeroth Corporation in columnar form for both years.

Exercise E15-7 (File 15e-7) Compute selected ratios

Bobbette Company has the following comparative balance sheet data:

BOBBETTE COMPANY
Comparative Balance Sheets
December 31

Assets	2002	2001
Cash	$15,000	$30,000
Receivables (Net)	65,000	60,000
Inventories	60,000	50,000
Plant assets (Net)	205,000	180,000
Total	$345,000	$320,000
Liabilities and Stockholders' equity		
Accounts payable	$50,000	$60,000
Mortgage payable (15%)	100,000	100,000
Common stock	140,000	120,000
Retained earnings	55,000	40,000
Total	$345,000	$320,000

Additional information for 2002:
  (1) Net income was $25,000.
  (2) Sales on account were $420,000. Sales returns and allowances were $20,000.
  (3) Cost of goods sold was $198,000.
  (4) Net cash provided by operating activities was $33,000.

Instructions:
Compute the following ratios at December 31, 2002:

(a)	Current ratio	**(e)**	Cash returns on sales
(b)	Acid test (quick) ratio	**(f)**	Cash debt coverage ratio
(c)	Receivables turnover	**(g)**	Current cash debt coverage ratio
(d)	Inventory turnover		

PROBLEMS

Problem P15-5A (File 15p-5a) Compute selected ratios, and compare liquidity, profitability, and solvency for two companies

Selected financial data of two intense competitors is a recent year are presented below:

	(in millions)	
	Kmart Corporation	Wal-Mart Stores, Inc.
Income Statement Data for Year		
Net sales	$34,025	$82,494
Cost of goods sold	25,992	65,586
Selling and administrative expenses	7,701	12,858
Interest expense	494	706
Other income (Net)	572	918
Income taxes	114	1,581
Net income	$296	$2,681
Balance Sheet Data (End of Year)		
Current assets	$9,187	$15,338
Property, plant, and equipment (Net)	7,842	17,481
Total assets	$17,029	$32,819
Current liabilities	$5,626	$9,973
Long-term debt	5,371	10,120
Total stockholders' equity	6,032	12,726
Total liabilities and stockholders' equity	$17,029	$32,819
Beginning-of-Year Balances		
Total assets	$17,504	$26,441
Total stockholders' equity	60,930	10,753
Other data:		
Average net receivables	1,570	695
Average inventory	7,317	12,539
Net cash provided by operating activities	351	3,106
Average current liabilities	5,720	10,110
Average total liabilities	11,230	20,160

Instructions:

(a) For each company, compute the following ratios:

(1)	Current ratio	(7)	Return on common stockholders' equity
(2)	Receivables turnover	(8)	Debt to total assets

(3)	Inventory turnover	(9)	Times interest earned
(4)	Profit margin	(10)	Current cash debt coverage ratio
(5)	Asset turnover	(11)	Cash returns on sales
(6)	Return on assets	(12)	Cash debt coverage ratio

(b) Compare the liquidity, profitability, and solvency of the two companies.

Problem P15-7A (File 15p-7a) Compute missing information given a set of ratios

Presented below is an incomplete income statement and an incomplete comparative balance sheet of Windsor Corporation:

WINDSOR CORPORATION
Income Statement
For the Year Ended December 31, 2003

Sales	$11,000,000
Cost of goods sold	?
Gross profit	?
Operating expenses	1,665,000
Income from operations	?
Other expenses and losses	
Interest expense	?
Income before income taxes	?
Income tax expense	560,000
Net income	?

WINDSOR CORPORATION
Balance Sheet
December 31

Assets	2003	2002
Current assets		
Cash	$450,000	$375,000
Accounts receivable (net)	?	950,000
Inventory	?	1,720,000
Total current assets	?	3,045,000
Plant assets (net)	4,620,000	3,955,000
Total assets	?	$7,000,000
Liabilities and stockholders' equity		
Current liabilities	?	$825,000
Long-term notes payable	?	2,800,000
Total liabilities	?	3,625,000
Common stock, $1 par	3,000,000	3,000,000
Retained earnings	400,000	375,000
Total stockholders' equity	3,400,000	3,375,000
Total liabilities and stockholders' equity	?	$7,000,000

Additional data:

1. The receivables turnover for 2003 is	10	times.
2. All sales are on account.		
3. The profit margin for 2003 is	14.50%	
4. Return on assets for 2003 is	22%	
5. The current ratio on December 31, 2003 is	3.2	
6. The inventory turnover for 2003 is	4.8	times.

Instructions:

Compute the missing information given the ratios above. Show computations. (*Note:* Start with one ratio and derive as much information as possible from it before trying another ratio. List all missing amounts under the ratio used to find the information.)

Problem P15-2B (File 15p-2b) Compute ratios from balance sheet and income statement

The comparative statements of Thoroughbred Company are presented below:

THOROUGHBRED COMPANY
Income Statement
For the Year Ended December 31

	2002	2001
Net sales	$660,000	$624,000
Cost of good sold	440,000	405,600
Gross profit	220,000	218,400
Selling and administrative expenses	143,880	149,760
Income from operations	76,120	68,640
Other expenses and losses		
Interest expense	7,920	7,200
Income before income taxes	68,200	61,440
Income tax expense	25,300	24,000
Net income	$42,900	$37,440

THOROUGHBRED COMPANY
Balance Sheet
December 31

Assets	2002	2001
Current assets		
Cash	$23,100	$21,600
Marketable securities	34,800	33,000
Accounts receivable (net)	106,200	93,800
Inventory	72,400	64,000
Total current assets	236,500	212,400
Plant assets (net)	465,300	459,600
Total assets	$701,800	$672,000

Liabilities and Stockholders' Equity

Current liabilities		
Accounts payable	$134,200	$132,000
Income taxes payable	25,300	24,000
Total current liabilities	159,500	156,000
Bonds payable	132,000	120,000
Total liabilities	291,500	276,000
Stockholders' equity		
Common stock ($10 par)	140,000	150,000
Retained earnings	270,300	246,000
Total stockholders' equity	410,300	396,000
Total liabilities and stockholders' equity	$701,800	$672,000

(1) On July 1, 2002, 1,000 shares of common stock were repurchased and canceled.
(2) All sales were on account.
(3) Net cash provided by operating activities was $36,000.

Instructions:
   (a) Compute the earnings per share (weighted average).
   (b) Compute the return on common stockholders' equity.
   (c) Compute the return on assets.
   (d) Compute the Current ratio.
   (e) Compute the Acid test (quick) ratio.
   (f) Compute the Receivables turnover.
   (g) Compute the Inventory turnover.
   (h) Compute times interest earned.
   (i) Compute asset turnover.
   (j) Compute debt to assets for
   (k) Compute the Current cash debt coverage ratio.
   (l) Compute the Cash returns on sales.
   (m) Compute the Cash debt coverage ratio.

Problem P15-6B (File 15p-6b) Compute missing information given a set of ratios

Presented below is an incomplete income statement and an incomplete comparative balance sheet of Percheron Corporation:

PERCHERON CORPORATION
Income Statement
For the Year Ended December 31, 2002

Sales	?
Cost of goods sold	4,200,000
Gross profit	?
Operating expenses	?
Income from operations	840,000
Other expenses and losses	
Interest expense	?
Income before income taxes	?
Income tax expense	?
Net income	$372,000

PERCHERON CORPORATION
Balance Sheet
December 31

Assets	2003	2002
Current assets		
Cash	$385,000	$299,978
Accounts receivable (net)	?	665,000
Inventory	?	1,204,000
Total current assets	?	2,168,978
Plant assets (net)	3,234,000	2,800,000
Total assets	?	$4,968,978
Liabilities and stockholders' equity		
Current liabilities	?	$824,978
Long-term notes payable	?	1,743,000
Total liabilities	?	2,567,978
Common stock, $1 par	2,100,000	2,100,000
Retained earnings	280,000	301,000
Total stockholders' equity	2,380,000	2,401,000
Total liabilities and stockholders' equity	?	$4,968,978

Additional information:
   (1) Times interest earned for 2002 is 8 times.
   (2) Net cash provided by operating activities for 2002 is $840,000.
   (3) Cash return on sales for 2002 is 14%.
   (4) The inventory turnover for 2002 is 4.2 times.
   (5) Asset turnover for 2002 was 1.2 times.
   (6) Working capital for 2002 was $1,344,000.

Instructions:

Compute the missing information given the ratios above. Show computations. (Note: Start with one ratio and derive as much information as possible from it before trying another ratio. List all missing amounts under the ratio used to find the information.)

APPENDIX D

PAYROLL ACCOUNTING

CHAPTER OUTLINE

CLUES, HINTS, AND TIPS

Drawing on worksheets

The first and foremost item to remember in this section is that most, if not all, of these items are "on top" of the worksheet. They are not in cells or attached to cells. You can enter data beneath them and around them without a problem. To bring up the Excel drawing tool bar right click on any menu bar and select Drawing from the options. On the drawing tool bar Excel gives you many preformatted and adjustable capabilities as well as some degree of free hand modifications. The drawing tool bar is shown here with the standard or default options. The first item to be addressed is the ability to draw arrows. To draw an arrow, click on the arrow icon and then click on the point where you want the arrow to appear to be coming from. If the point of origin is not visible on the screen after you activate the arrow, use the scroll bars to navigate the worksheet or hit escape two or more times to cancel the draw arrow command while you reposition the screen. Place your cursor over the point of origin and click the left mouse button down once and hold it down. Now move the mouse cursor to the destination or target, if the target is not visible on the screen move your mouse cursor towards the general direction and Excel will scroll towards it. When you have what will be the arrowhead in position, release the mouse button and the arrow will form. If the "weight" or thickness of the line is other than what you want, while the arrow is still "active" as indicated by empty circles at each end, click into the icon with the numerous different thickness lines and pick your choice. If the texture of the arrow is less than desirable, while the arrow is still active, click into the textures icon, usually next to the weight icon, and pick your choice.

Once the arrow is drawn, place your cursor back on top of it and move the cursor slightly until you get a four headed arrow for a cursor. At the point that the cursor changes, left click the mouse to "grab" the arrow then right click it and a pop-up menu will appear. From this menu select Edit Points. With this option active, you can place your cursor on the arrow at any point and bend it around. To flex the arrow, move your cursor over the arrow and when it becomes a "crosshairs" type presentation, left mouse button down and drag it around. The point of origin and the destination will remain the same but the path will change. If the corners are abrupt, place your cursor on a corner, right click the arrow to get the pop-up menu and select Smooth points. From this point on your corners should be rounded. If you place your cursor over a corner point, shown only while the arrow is in edit mode, you will see a "line handle" appear, grabbing and moving this line handle changes the aspects of the corner. When you have an arrow or line selected, they work the same; you can change the weight, pattern, and color through the icons on the drawing bar. On the chapter data file, appendixd, there is an arrow tab with some random drawings and features.

There is a text box on the tool bar, it is a white sheet of paper with a letter "A" in the upper left corner and lines making it appear like a newspaper. Click on this icon and then click into the worksheet and keep holding the left mouse button down. While you are holding the mouse button down, drag the cursor away from the point of origin to create a text box. At any time you can drop the drag and start to enter text into the box. If the box was created to wrong size, click near the borders to get the handles or ears active, then grab a handle or ear and drag it to a bigger size. To move the box, select the box, then move your cursor near the edge until it becomes a four arrow headed object, then left mouse button down and drag it to the new location. Just like dragging other objects like arrows and lines. Spell check will check the spelling inside text boxes, just like inside comments. You can fill the box by selecting it and then selecting a fill color. You can change its borders by selecting the box and selecting a line weight and texture from the tool bar. Many of the screen prints in this booklet were done with text boxes and arrows from the drawing tool bar.

There are preformatted rectangles and ovals on the drawing tool bar. Simply click on the icon then click into the worksheet and start to drag them around until you get the shape you want. You can drag them to a new location by moving your cursor near an edge looking for the four headed arrow before clicking down, just like arrows, lines, and text boxes.

To delete an object, select it and hit the delete key. Using the cut command will allow you to paste it somewhere else – once. Using the copy command will allow you to paste it in numerous locations.

On the tool bar and through the path Insert>Picture you can insert onto the worksheet pictures from clip art or your own personal albums. This is a great feature to document fixed assets or merchandise for inventory type issues but the file sizes get large very quickly. Word art is also available for use through the drawing tool bar are well as the path Insert>Picture>WordArt. And do not miss the opportunity to play with the Insert Diagram or organizational chart tool These tools can be very effective when used well. As recommended earlier in booklet, view professional magazines, newspapers, and text books to get examples of good presentation techniques. None of the examples here would be used in a professional format, they are provided as examples of the power (and abuse of power) available in Excel.

EXERCISES

Exercise ED-3 (File de-3) Prepare payroll register and record payroll and payroll tax expense

Martinez Company has the following data for the weekly payroll ending January, 31:

Employee	Hours per weekday M	T	W	T	F	S	Hourly rate	Federal Inc Tax Withheld	Health Ins
M. Miller	8	8	9	8	10	3	$10.00	$34.00	$10.00
E. Neupert	8	8	8	8	8	2	12.00	37.00	15.00
K. Mann	9	10	8	8	9		13.00	58.00	15.00

Employees are paid 1 1/2 times the regular hourly rate for all hours worked in excess of 40 hours per week. FICA taxes are 8% on the first $65,000 of gross earnings. Martinez Company is subject to 5.4% state unemployment taxes and 0.8% federal unemployment taxes on the first $7,000 of gross earnings.
Instructions:
(a) Prepare the payroll register for the weekly payroll.
(b) Prepare the journal entries to record the payroll and Martinez's payroll liabilities.

PROBLEMS

Problem PD-2A (File dp-2a) Prepare payroll register and payroll entries

Happy Hardware has four employees who are paid on an hourly basis plus time-and-a-half for all hours worked in excess of 40 hours a week. Payroll data for the week ended March 15, 2002, are presented below:

Employee	Hours worked	Hourly rate	Federal Inc Tax Withheld	United Fund
Joe McKane	40	$14.00	??	$5
Mary Miller	42	13.00	??	$5
Andy Manion	44	13.00	$60	$8
Kim Cheng	46	13.00	$51	$5

McKane and Miller are married. They claim 0 and 4 withholding allowances respectively. The following tax rates are applicable:

FICA	8.0%
State income tax	3.0%
State unemployment taxes	5.4%
Federal unemployment taxes	0.8%

The first three employees are sales clerks (store wages expense). The fourth employee performs administrative duties (office wages expense.)

Instructions:

(a) Prepare a payroll register for the weekly payroll using the wage-bracket withholding table below:

(b) Journalize the payroll on March 15, 2002, and the accrual of employer payroll taxes.

(c) Journalize the payment of the payroll on March 16, 2002.

(d) Journalize the deposit in a Federal Reserve bank on March 31, 2002, of the FICA and federal income taxes payable to the government.

Problem PD-2B (File dp-2b) Prepare payroll register and payroll entries

Paris Drug Store has four employees who are paid on an hourly basis plus time-and-a-half for all hours worked in excess of a 40 hour week.

Payroll data for the week ended February 15, 2002, are presented below:

Employee	Hours worked	Hourly rate	Federal Inc Tax Withheld	United Fund
L. Scott	39	$13.00	???	$0
S. Stahl	42	$12.00	???	$5
M. Rasheed	44	$12.00	$61	$8
L. Quick	46	$12.00	$49	$5

Scott and Stahl are married. They claim 2 and 4 withholding allowances, respectively. The following tax rates are applicable:

FICA	8.0%
State income tax	3.0%
State unemployment taxes	5.4%
Federal unemployment taxes	0.8%

The first three employees are sales clerks (store wages expense). The fourth employee performs administrative duties (office wages expense.)

Instructions:

Prepare a payroll register for the weekly payroll using the wage-bracket withholding table below:

Married persons - WEEKLY Payroll Period (For Wages Paid in 2002)							
If the wages are -		and the number of withholding allowances claimed is -					
At least	But less than	0	1	2	3	4	5	6
		The amount of income tax to be withheld is -						
490	500	56	48	40	32	24	17	9
500	510	57	49	42	34	26	18	10
510	520	59	51	43	35	27	20	12
520	530	60	52	45	37	29	21	13
530	540	62	54	46	38	30	23	15
540	550	63	55	48	40	32	24	16
550	560	65	57	49	41	33	26	18
560	570	66	58	51	43	35	27	19
570	580	68	60	52	44	36	29	21
580	590	69	61	54	46	38	30	22
590	600	71	63	55	47	39	32	24
600	610	82	64	57	49	41	33	25
610	620	74	66	58	50	42	35	27

(b) Journalize the payroll on February 15, 2002, and the accrual of employer payroll taxes.

(c) Journalize the payment of the payroll on March 16, 2002.

(d) Journalize the deposit in a Federal Reserve Bank on March 31, 2002, of the FICA and federal income taxes payable to the government.

A

B

C

D

E

F

G

H

I

S

T

Today and Now, 37

U

Undo and Redo, 12
Units of activity, 74

V

Vlookup, 93